Java for the
Beginning Programmer

Java for the
Beginning Programmer

by Jeff Heaton

Heaton Research, Inc.
St. Louis

Java for the Beginning Programmer, First Edition

First printing

Publisher: Heaton Research, Inc

Author: Jeff Heaton

Editor: Mary McKinnis

ISBN: 0-9773206-1-8

SOFTWARE LICENSE AGREEMENT: TERMS AND CONDITIONS

The media and/or any online materials accompanying this book that are available now or in the future contain programs and/or text files (the "Software") to be used in connection with this book. Heaton Research, Inc. hereby grants to you a license to use and distribute software programs that make use of the compiled binary form of this book's source code. You may not redistribute the source code contained in this book, without the written permission of Heaton Research, Inc. Your purchase, acceptance, or use of the Software will constitute your acceptance of such terms.

The Software compilation is the property of Heaton Research, Inc. unless otherwise indicated and is protected by copyright to Heaton Research, Inc. or other copyright owner(s) as indicated in the media files (the "Owner(s)"). You are hereby granted a license to use and distribute the Software for your personal, noncommercial use only. You may not reproduce, sell, distribute, publish, circulate, or commercially exploit the Software, or any portion thereof, without the written consent of Heaton Research, Inc. and the specific copyright owner(s) of any component software included on this media.

In the event that the Software or components include specific license requirements or end-user agreements, statements of condition, disclaimers, limitations or warranties ("End-User License"), those End-User Licenses supersede the terms and conditions herein as to that particular Software component. Your purchase, acceptance, or use of the Software will constitute your acceptance of such End-User Licenses.

By purchase, use or acceptance of the Software, you further agree to comply with all export laws and regulations of the United States as such laws and regulations may exist from time to time.

SOFTWARE SUPPORT

Components of the supplemental Software and any offers associated with them may be supported by the specific Owner(s) of that material but they are not supported by Heaton Research, Inc.. Information regarding any available support may be obtained from the Owner(s) using the information provided in the appropriate README files or listed elsewhere on the media.

Should the manufacturer(s) or other Owner(s) cease to offer support or decline to honor any offer, Heaton Research, Inc. bears no responsibility. This notice concerning support for the Software is provided for your information only. Heaton Research, Inc. is not the agent or principal of the Owner(s), and Heaton Research, Inc. is in no way responsible for providing any support for the Software, nor is it liable or responsible for any support provided, or not provided, by the Owner(s).

WARRANTY

Heaton Research, Inc. warrants the enclosed media to be free of physical defects for a period of ninety (90) days after purchase. The Software is not available from Heaton Research, Inc. in any other form or media than that enclosed herein or posted to www.heaton-research.com. If you discover a defect in the media during this warranty period, you may obtain a replacement of identical format at no charge by sending the defective media, postage prepaid, with proof of purchase to:

```
Heaton Research, Inc.
Customer Support Department
1734 Clarkson Rd #107
Chesterfield, MO 63017-4976

Web: www.heatonresearch.com
E-Mail: support@heatonresearch.com
```

After the 90-day period, you can obtain replacement media of identical format by sending us the defective disk, proof of purchase, and a check or money order for $10, payable to Heaton Research, Inc..

DISCLAIMER

Heaton Research, Inc. makes no warranty or representation, either expressed or implied, with respect to the Software or its contents, quality, performance, merchantability, or fitness for a particular purpose. In no event will Heaton Research, Inc., its distributors, or dealers be liable to you or any other party for direct, indirect, special, incidental, consequential, or other damages arising out of the use of or inability to use the Software or its contents even if advised of the possibility of such damage. In the event that the Software includes an online update feature, Heaton Research, Inc. further disclaims any obligation to provide this feature for any specific duration other than the initial posting.

The exclusion of implied warranties is not permitted by some states. Therefore, the above exclusion may not apply to you. This warranty provides you with specific legal rights; there may be other rights that you may have that vary from state to state. The pricing of the book with the Software by Heaton Research, Inc. reflects the allocation of risk and limitations on liability contained in this agreement of Terms and Conditions.

SHAREWARE DISTRIBUTION

This Software may contain various programs that are distributed as shareware. Copyright laws apply to both shareware and ordinary commercial software, and the copyright Owner(s) retains all rights. If you try a shareware program and continue using it, you are expected to register it. Individual programs differ on details of trial periods, registration, and payment. Please observe the requirements stated in appropriate files.

This book is dedicated to all of my Java students. Both students from traditional classrooms, as well as electronic.

Acknowledgments

There are several people who I would like to thank. First, I would like to thank my Java students over the years. Much of this books material was developed for classroom teaching and improved over years of classroom use.

I would like to thank Mary McKinnis for editing the book. I would also like to thank Mary McKinnis for trying out the book examples and offering many helpful suggestions.

I would like to thank my sister Carrie Spear for layout and formatting suggestions.

Contents at a Glance

Contents

Table of Figures

XXII   Java for the Beginning Programmer

Table of Tables

Table of Listings

INTRODUCTION

Java for the Beginning Programmer teaches Java to someone with absolutely no programming background. This book focuses on core programming topics such as variables, looping, subroutines, and program layout. This course focuses on real programming techniques, and not using an Integrated Development Environment (IDE) to generate code. This course ends with an introduction to graphical user interface programming.

Prerequisites
There are none! This book starts from the very beginning

By focusing on core programming techniques, and not using an IDE to generate code, the programmer is given a solid foundation in the Java programming language. This book prepares the reader for more advanced Java study, or one of our other Java programming books.

Each chapter includes review questions and an assignment. This book can be used either as a college text book, or for independent reading. This book was compiled from the author's years of experience teaching the Java programming language.

CHAPTER 1: INTRODUCTION TO JAVA

Welcome to the book "Java for the Beginning Programmer". In this book you will be introduced to the Java programming language. This book will cover topics such as:

Prerequisites
There are none! This book starts from the very beginning

- **Java Programming Syntax**
- **Basic Object Oriented Programming (OOP)**
- **Creating Console-Mode applications**
- **Java Programming Fundamentals**

After you complete this book you will be ready to create basic Java applications or go on to a more advanced Java course or book.

Prerequisites

This book assumes no prior programming experience. It is only assumed that you know how to use a Windows/Mac computer and the Internet. A very basic knowledge of Algebra may also be useful. All of the screen shots in this book were made using Windows XP. Other systems, such as Mac or Linux will look slightly different.

Getting Started

The objective for the first chapter is to get a basic Java application entered, compiled and executed. You will be shown how to obtain and install Java. You will then be shown how to enter your source code. Finally, I will show you how to compile and execute your application. These basic steps will be repeated through this book as you create and test applications of your own. So it is very important that you understand this process. To summarize, the primary topics of Chapter 1 are:

- Introduction to the Java Language
- Compiling a Java Application
- Running a Java Application
- What is Java

Java is a programming language developed by Sun Microsystems. The Java programming language can be obtained free-of-charge from Sun Microsystems's website http://java.sun.com. Java syntax builds upon C/C++ syntax. If you are familiar with the C/C++ programming languages, Java will seem very familiar.

However, unlike C/C++, Java is very cross-platform. By cross-platform, I mean that a Java program will run on many different operating systems. You could easily take a Java application and run it on a Windows, Mac OS-X, or a Linux based computer. This often requires no change to the program or even recompiling.

Java is also Object Oriented. If you have never programmed an object-oriented language before, this will probably be one of the most difficult aspects of Java for you to learn. Object Oriented programming will be discussed in Chapter 13. In essence, Object Oriented programs are broken up into reusable objects.

Java provides several different application types to fit different programming needs. Next, I will explain the different types of Java applications.

Types of Java Applications

Learning Objective #1
There are three types of Java application: console, GUI and applet.

In this book you will learn to create several different types of Java applications. These application types appear quite differently to the user. Picking the correct application type is an important part of the Java development process. There are three types of Java application:

- Java Console Applications
- Java GUI Applications
- Java Applets

Most of what you learn in this class can be applied to any of the above application types. However, there are some differences in the way you program each. I will begin by explaining the differences and similarities between each of these. This book will focus primarily on console applications.

Java Console Application

A Java Console application can only display textual data. Console applications resemble DOS based applications in that all interaction with the program is through keyboard and text output. The mouse, and any use of multiple windows is not supported.

Console applications are good for applications that have limited interaction with the user. If a program must run in the background, away from the user, a console application is an ideal choice. Console applications are also great for setting up quick tests to see how Java works. The applications you develop in this book will be console applications.

Background applications are almost always written as console applications. A background application is a program that runs, often for a long period of time, without user interaction. Examples of background applications include:

- Anti-virus programs that scan while the user is using the computer
- Business Data processing/loading applications that process large volumes of data

Figure 1.1 shows a Java Console application.

Console Applications
Look like command
prompt or terminal
windows.

Figure 1.1: A Console Application

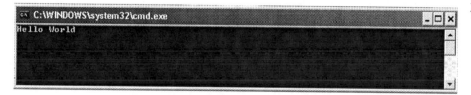

When to use a Console Application

- Limited user interaction
- Applications that run in the background
- Quick test applications to try out techniques in Java

Limitations of a Console Application

- No mouse support
- No graphical/window support
- No additional windows

For some applications, you will need to interact with the user through Windows. In these cases, you should choose a GUI application over a console application.

Java GUI Application

Most applications used with windows are regular Graphical User Interface, or GUI applications. Java allows you to create a GUI application that takes advantage of a rich set of window and control types. If you are going to create an application that the user works directly with, you will most likely want to create a GUI application.

This book will provide a brief introduction into Java applications that make use of Windows. You will be shown how to do this using Java Swing. Swing is Java's latest release of their windowing system for the Java language. Figure 1.2 shows a Java GUI Application.

GUI Applications
Look like regular
Windows applications.

Figure 1.2: Java GUI Application

When to use a GUI Application

- Working directly with the user
- Applications that must display graphical information

Limitations of a GUI Application

- More complex to setup than console application
- Less convenient to run in the background

Java Applet

Java Applets allow you to imbed a program directly into a browser. The user simply has to visit your website to view the applet. Applets can be used to display graphics, animation and produce sound/music. Applets can be very useful for displaying advertisements on web sites or providing a greater deal of interactivity than an HTML page alone can provide.

Although applets can be used for a variety of multimedia purposes, they are rarely used for this purpose. Macromedia Flash is the more common choice for animation/multimedia web applications. Additionally, Microsoft Internet Explorer, currently the most popular browser, does not include support for the latest version of Java applets, by default. Due to these factors, the use of applets has become somewhat restricted in the last few years.

Because an applet runs in the web browser, an applet cannot make changes to the user's local computer. This means that it is difficult for an applet to save any information entered by the user. The applet does not have the option of saving files on the user's computer. The only thing that an applet can do with entered data is to submit it back to the website.

This book will not cover Java Applets. Figure 1.3 shows a Java applet.

Java Applet
Applets run from within an Internet browser.

Figure 1.3: A Java Applet

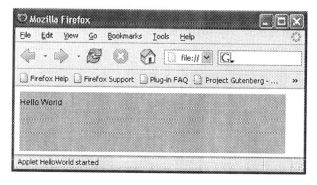

When to use a Java Applet

- When your application should run directly with a website
- When your application enhances the use of a website
- Applications that display animation that should be quickly accessed form a website

Limitations of a Java Applet

- Applets cannot save data to the user's disk
- Applets can not make use of the latest Java technology on Internet Explorer.

Cross Platform

Java is also cross platform. This means that a Java application can be run on a variety of computer systems, without any modification to the program. Java runs on many different platforms, but some of the more common ones include:

- Microsoft Windows
- Apple Macintosh
- Linux
- Cell phones and other embedded devices

Consider the program running in Figure 1.4. This is a Java application running under Windows XP. As you can see, it contains buttons, graphics and other features you would normally expect from a program. This application is written in Java, so it can run on systems other than Windows. You can see this program running under Windows in Figure 1.4.

Figure 1.4: A Java Application Running on Windows

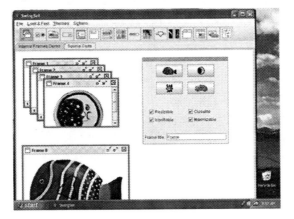

This exact same program can be run under the Macintosh. This takes no changes at all. I simply copied the application to a CD-ROM and loaded it onto a Mac. The program runs and looks very similar to the Windows version, except that it more closely matches how a Macintosh application should look. Java always attempts to match the look and feel of the operating system it is running on. You can see the program running under Mac in Figure 1.5.

Figure 1.5: A Java Application Running on the Macintosh

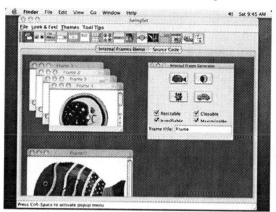

You can download everything you will need to develop in Java for free. Java can be downloaded from Sun Microsystems's site at http://java.sun.com. From this web page, choose the J2SE 5.0 option under the "Popular Downloads" section on the right side of your page.

Chapter Review

In this chapter you saw how to install a Java environment on your computer. This consisted of downloading NetBeans from Sun Microsystems and installing it. You were shown how to create a project in NetBeans to hold your first application.

There are three types of Java applications that will be covered in this book. Console Applications, which we saw in this chapter, communicate with text only. Java GUI Applications can have Windows and Forms. Applets are graphical applications that run inside of a web browser.

A very simple program was introduced to show how to execute a console mode application from NetBeans. In the next class chapter, you will be shown how to create an application that makes decisions and processes data.

New Terms

Applet A Java application that runs from within a web browser.

Console Application A Java application that can only display text.

Cross Platform The ability for a program to run on more than one type of computer system.

GUI Application A Java application that uses Windows and the mouse.

Source Code The instructions that a programmer enters to create an application.

Review Questions

1. What do you call a programming language that will run on many different computer systems, such as Windows, Macintosh and Linux?

2. Which company produced Java?

3. Is Java Object Oriented or Cross platform?

4. What other language does Java's source code resemble?

5. What other programming language is often used in place of applets?

Assignment #1

You are to write a program that will process insurance policies for a large life insurance company. This program will be run nightly, and will sometimes process over 100,000 policies a night. You must write this program, but first, your manager wants to know what sort of application you would like to use for this job. Your choices are:

Java Console Application
Java Applet
Java GUI Application

Choose which application type you will use. Explain why you chose this type. Also explain why the other two were not suitable. Your answer should not be longer than two paragraphs.

CHAPTER 2: INSTALLING, COMPILING AND RUNNING

In Chapter 2 you will learn about:
- **Installing Java**
- **Entering your First Program**
- **Running your First Program**
- **Installing Java**

In this chapter you will learn how to install Java and create your first Java application. Java installation is easy. There are two steps to this.

- Downloading and installing Java
- Setting up Java's path

You will be shown how to do this in the next sections.

Downloading Java and Installing Java

First you have to download Java. Java can be downloaded free of charge from Sun Microsystems. Type the following URL into a browser to be taken to Sun Microsystem's Java page.

```
http://java.sun.com/
```

Once you access Sun's Java page you must make your way to the download page. Sun changes this page around from time to time, so the download instructions and screens shown here may not match 100%. On the right side of the page you will likely see a section called "Popular Downloads". Select J2SE 5.0. If there is a version later than 5.0, choose it. This will take you to a page that looks similar to Figure 2.1.

Figure 2.1: Select Java Version to Download

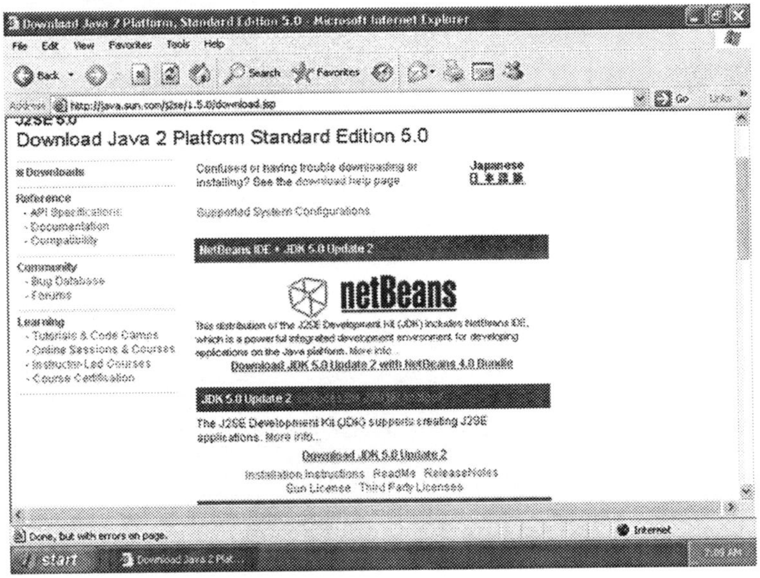

Which one?
Choose JDK.

This allows you to select how you would like to download Java. You have two choices.

- NetBeans IDE + JDK
- JDK

For this book we only need the JDK. So select the second section (after the NetBeans section), as seen near the bottom of Figure 2.1. Once you select your download you will be presented with the software license, which you must accept. You can see the software license in Figure 2.2.

Figure 2.2: Accept the License Agreement

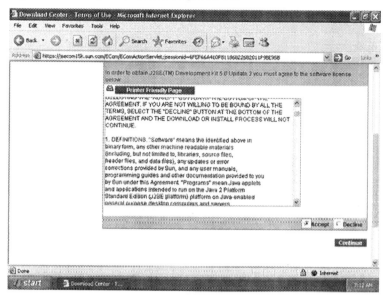

Once you accept you will be taken to another page where you can choose how you download the Windows version. There are two choices:

- Windows Offline Installation
- Windows Online Installation

Either of these installations will work just fine. If you were going to install Java on a large number of machines it would make sense to download the off-line version and copy that file to each machine. Installing to a single machine, as you are likely doing, the online version makes more sense. The online version can resume downloads if anything goes wrong during the install. Choose the online installation, when presented with Figure 2.3.

Which one?
It does not matter a great deal, but choose offline.

Figure 2.3: Choose Windows Online Install

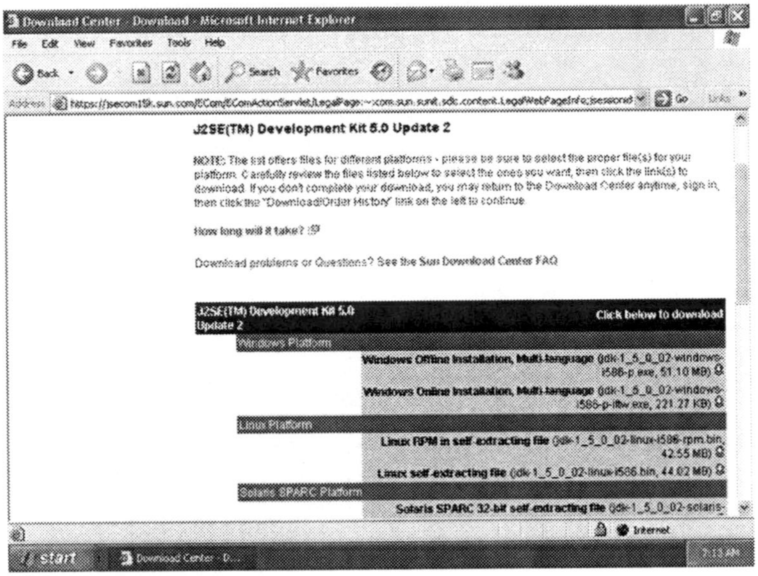

Learning Objective #2
Install Java.

The download will now begin. Your web browser will display one or more "Security Warning" pages, such as seen in Figure 2.4. Security warnings come up whenever you are installing new software, and in this case, installing new software is exactly what we are doing. Click the "Run" button. If you are using a browser other than Microsoft Internet Explorer, this button may be named "Open".

Figure 2.4: Run the Program you Downloaded

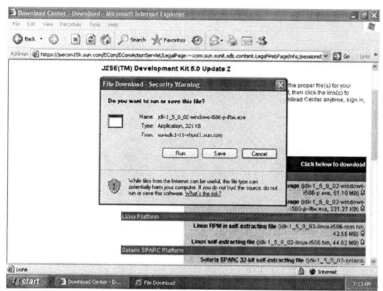

You will have to accept a second license agreement shown in Figure 2.5. Click "Next" to continue.

Figure 2.5: Accept this License Agreement

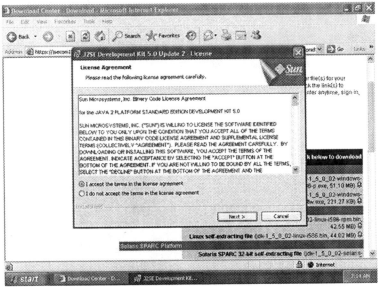

You will now be presented with some installation options, as seen in Figure 2.6. Accept all of these by clicking "Next".

Figure 2.6: Standard Install

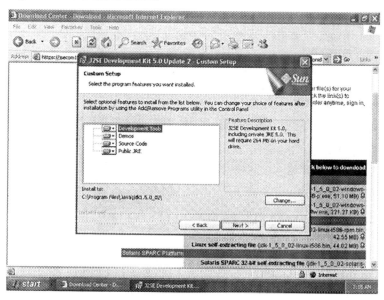

The install program will now download the required files, as seen in Figure 2.7. Wait for the progress bar to reach 100%.

Figure 2.7: Install Underway

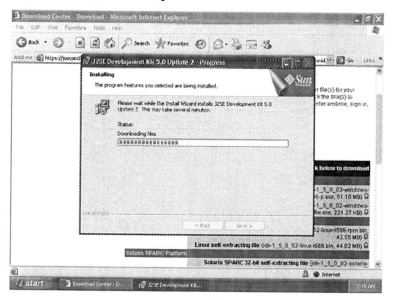

Once the download completes you will be presented with the features you can choose from. You should leave everything as it is and click "Next", when you see Figure 2.8.

Figure 2.8: Accept Features

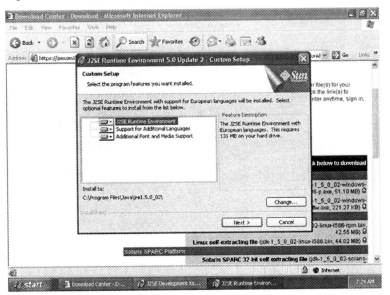

You will be asked with which browsers you wish to integrate Java, as seen in Figure 2.9. You should leave everything checked and click next. This allows your browsers to make use of Java.

Figure 2.9: Browser Registration

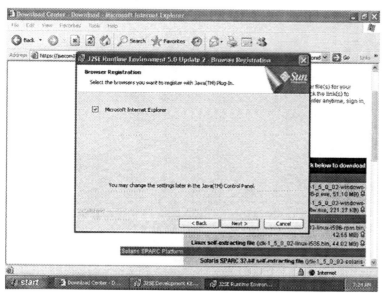

Once you choose these options installation begins. You can see the installation process in Figure 2.10. Wait for the progress bar to reach 100%.

Figure 2.10: Installing Java

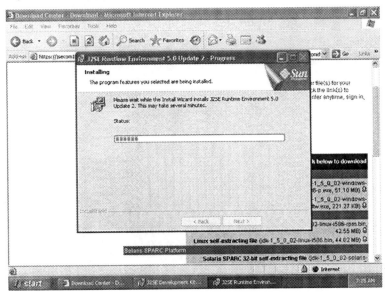

Once the bar reaches 100%, Java installation is complete. You will now see Figure 2.11. Click "Finish".

Figure 2.11: Install Complete

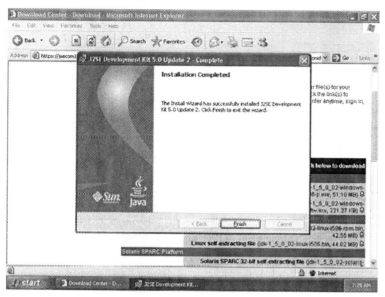

You have now installed Java. But you are not finished yet. To use Java in this book, you must add Java to your system path. This is covered in the next section.

Setting up Java's Path

Once you install Java you must setup the path so that the computer can find Java. To do this you must first obtain the path that Java is stored at. This path is a string such as "C:\Program Files\Java\jdk1.5.0_01\bin". The easiest way to get this path is to use Windows explorer. Launch Windows Explorer (Either by pressing your Windows button and "E" at the same time, or by launching it from the "Start Menu") then navigate to your Java BIN directory, as seen in Figure 2.12.

Learning Objective #3
Setup Java's path.

Figure 2.12: Get the Java Path

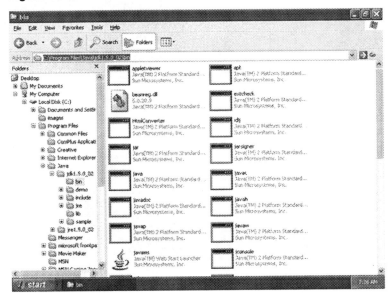

Once you reach the Java BIN directory, your path will be in the "Address Bar", as seen above. Select this address and choose "Copy" from the "Edit" menu. Your path has been saved to the clipboard.

Now you must bring up the control panel to insert this path. Click the Windows XP Start button and choose "Control Panel". You may start in "Windows XP" mode, as seen in Figure 2.13. Choose "Switch to Classic View".

Figure 2.13: Windows XP Control Panels

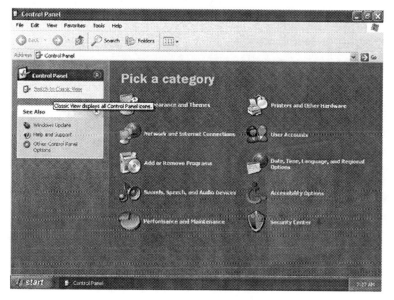

Control Panels
Switch to
classic view.

Once you switch to Classic View you will see Figure 2.14. Double click the "System" icon.

Figure 2.14: Classic Control Panels

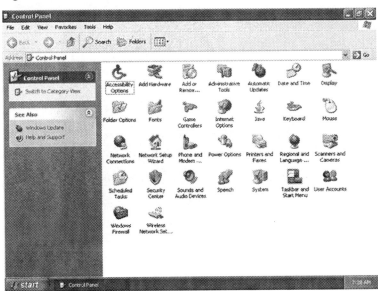

Double clicking the "System" icon will bring you to Figure 2.15. Choose the "Advanced" tab.

Figure 2.15: System Properties

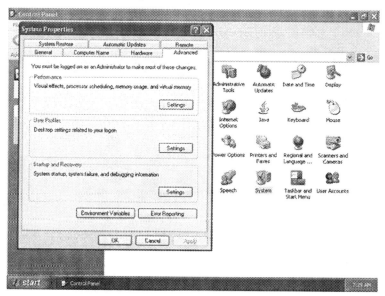

Click the "Environment Variables" button. This will take you to Figure 2.16.

Figure 2.16: Environmental Variables

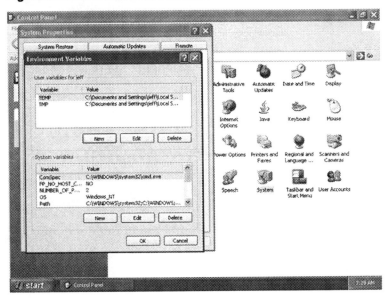

This will allow you to see the user variables for your user account. We will be adding a variable named PATH. Make sure you add it to the top section, and not the bottom.

If there is no PATH already click "Add" and add the path, as seen in Figure 2.17.

Figure 2.17: Set the Path

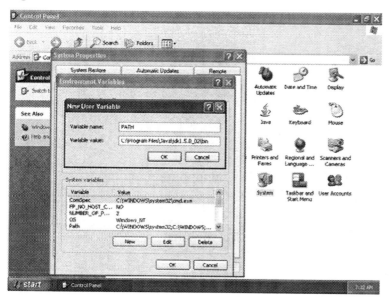

If there is already a variable named path then select it and click "Edit". You should then add the Java path onto the end of whatever is there. Make sure to put a semicolon (;) at the end of whatever was there. i.e., if there was already c:\;c:\windows. You would modify it to be something such as c:\;c:\windows;C:\Program Files\Java\jdk1.5.0_01\bin

Now click OK. You will have created a path to Java. Now we will test it.

Testing your Java Path

Open a command prompt window. This can be done from under the Windows XP Start button and then choosing "All Programs", then "Accessories", then "Command Prompt". From the command prompt enter:

```
java -version
```

You should see the version of Java displayed. Now enter:

```
javac -version
```

You should see the version again, and a long list of options. Both of these commands should produce a screen similar to Figure 2.18.

Figure 2.18: Verify Java Works

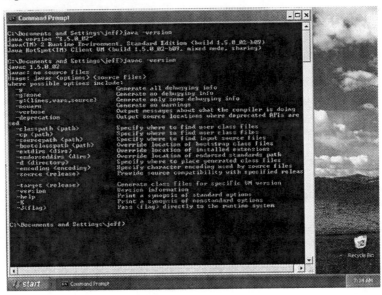

If you did everything right, you should see something like above. If you are getting errors, recheck the steps on setting the path.

Now that you have installed Java, you are ready to create your first Java application.

Compiling and Executing your Application

In this section you will create your first Java application. It is very important that you know how to do this properly. While reading this book you will create many Java applications. Future sections will not re-explain how to do this, therefore it is important that you see how to do this now. There are several steps:

- Create a directory to contain your application
- Enter your application
- Compile your application
- Run your application

This section will show you how to complete each of these steps. We will begin with creating a directory.

Creating a Directory

First you must create a directory to hold your application. Begin by opening a Command Prompt window. Make sure that you are on your C: drive, or whatever hard drive you wish to use. Do this by simply entering:

```
c:
```

Now create a directory to hold your projects:

```
md \JavaProjects
```

Now move into your new directory.

```
cd \JavaProjects
```

Then create a subdirectory for each chapter, such as:

```
md chapter1
md chapter2
```

Now enter chapter 2's directory:

```
cd chapter2
```

If done correctly you should now see Figure 2.19.

Learning Objective #4
Create a place to store your Java programs.

Figure 2.19: Create a Place to Put your First Application

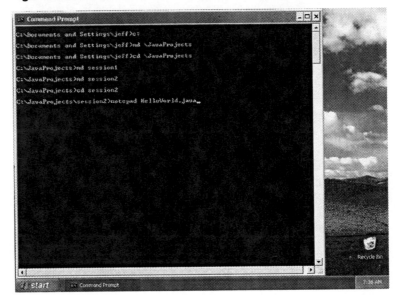

Now that you have a directory to hold your application, you must enter your application.

Enter your Application

For this book you will use Notepad to enter your application. To do this enter the command:

```
notepad HelloWorld.java
```

Make sure you enter this exactly as I have it. If you change which letters are capital, you will run into problems! This will start up Notepad and allow you to enter your source code. The source code is what makes up your program and is compiled into your final application. Once you enter the above command you will see Notepad launch and ask if you want to create a new file. You should choose "Yes", as seen in Figure 2.20.

Figure 2.20: Create your Source Code

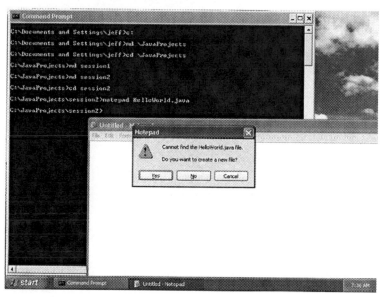

If you use notepad to re-open this file later, you will not be prompted to create the file, the file will simply open. Now that Notepad is open you should enter the application as seen in Figure 2.21.

Figure 2.21: Enter your Source Code

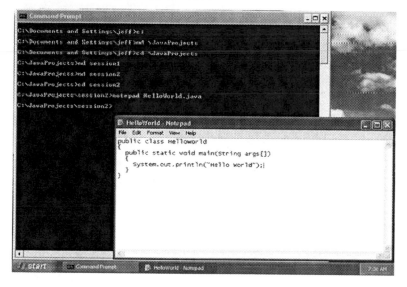

This program is shown in Listing 2.1.

Listing 2.1: Hello World! (HelloWorld.java)

Important
Notice the code line "class HelloWorld"; it must match the filename "HelloWorld.java".

```
public class HelloWorld
{
  public static void main(String args[])
  {
    System.out.println("Hello World");
  }
}
```

Once you have entered your program you will compile it, as shown in the next section.

One very important item to note is the class name. The class name above, in Listing 2.1, is HelloWorld. This must match the filename "HelloWorld.java".

Compile your Application

Now I will show you how to compile your application. To do this, return to the command prompt window and enter:

Learning Objective #5
Compile your program.

```
javac HelloWorld.java
```

This will compile your application. Compiling is the process by which your source code is changed into a form that the computer can understand. This is also where you will see compile errors if you have entered anything incorrectly. You can see a successful compile in Figure 2.22.

Figure 2.22: View the Class File

If you would like to see what the compiler created enter the command:

```
dir
```

This will show you a file called HelloWorld.class. This is the compiled form of your program that can be executed. You will see how to do this in the next section.

If you entered anything incorrectly, you will now get compile errors. If you did get a compile error or two, compare your source code to Listing 2.2. Each compile error will have a line number, such as (22), which will indicate which line number caused the error. For example, (22) would indicate an error on line number 22 of "HelloWorld.java".

Run your Application

If you have compiled without errors, now you are ready to run, or execute, your application. This is done by entering the command:

Learning Objective #6
Run your program.

```
java HelloWorld
```

This will run your program and display "Hello World" as seen in Figure 2.23.

Figure 2.23: Run the Example

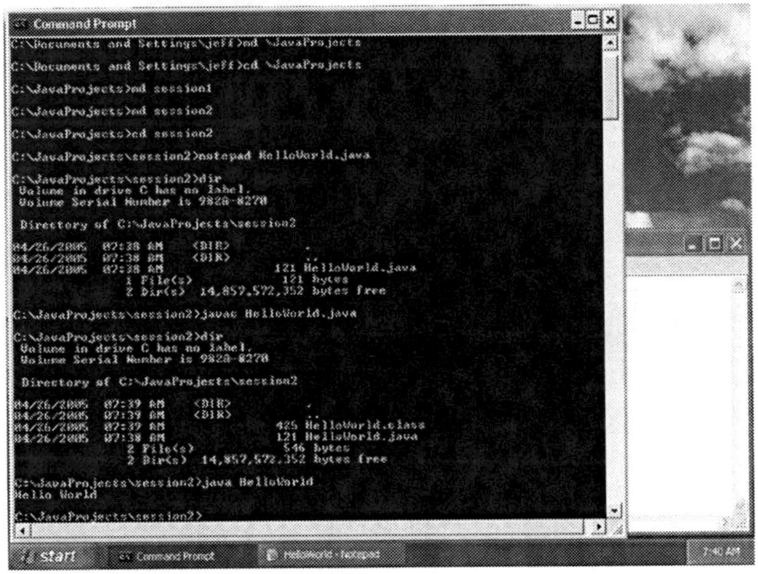

Congratulations! You have created and executed your first Java application.

Chapter Review

In this chapter you learned download and instal Java. You also had to setup the system path so that you could use Java from the command prompt. You then created your first application. This consisted of creating a directory to hold that application, entering the application, compiling the application, and then finally executing the application.

New Terms

.class A file type that holds a compiled Java program/class.

.java A file type that holds the source code for a Java program/class.

Compile When java source code is converted into a form that the computer can easily understand. This converts a .java file into a .class file.

Execute To start and run your program.

java The command to execute/run a Java application.

javac The command to compile a Java application.

Notepad A Windows application that can be used to edit source code.

Run When your Java program begins execution. Has the same meaning as execute.

Review Questions

1. What is the command to compile the source file "MyProgram.java"?

2. What is contained in a .class file?

3. What is the command to compile, and the command to run the Java source file "RunMe.java"?

4. What is a program that can be used to edit Java source files?

5. What must be done to a Java source file before it can be executed/ran?

Assignment #2

Create a program, named Assignment2.java that will display your name. This is primarily an exercise to make sure that you can compile and execute a Java application. Make sure you can both compile and execute, as this procedure will be repeated many times in this book.

Listing 2.1 will be helpful as a starting point, but make sure you change the class name to "Assignment2".

CHAPTER 3: VARIABLES

In Chapter 3 you will learn about:
- Java Program Structure
- Variables
- Conversions
- Displaying Data
- Formatting Numbers
- Java Program Structure

In the last chapter we created a simple Java application. This program did no more than display Hello World. Yet you were probably wondering what was behind up the Java source code that you entered to create the program. In the next section you will be introduced to what makes up a Java source code file.

Anatomy of a Java Program

Source code is what you "type in" to create a program. The compiler takes source code and creates a program from it that the computer can execute. As a programmer, it will be your job to create this source code. We used some simple source code in the previous section, now lets take a look at a slightly more complex program and see what goes into its source code.

Learning Objective #1
Structure of a
Java program.

Listing 3.1 shows a simple Java application that asks you what your name is, and then says hello to you.

Listing 3.1: Sample Java Program (UserInput.java)

```java
import java.io.*;

public class UserInput
{

  /**
   * Main entry point for example.
   * @param args Not used.
   */
  public static void main(String args[])
  {
    try
    {
```

```
BufferedReader userInput =
  new BufferedReader(
  new InputStreamReader(System.in));

System.out.print("What is your name? ");
String str = userInput.readLine();
System.out.println("Hello " + str);
}
catch(IOException e)
{
  System.out.println("IO Exception");
}
}
}
}
```

We will examine this program from the top, beginning with the import statements.

Import Statements

Look at the top of Listing 3.1, and you will see an import line. Import lines allow you to use information from other packages. Packages hold many source files together. When you have a large project it makes sense to break it up into smaller packages. In this book we will not create projects larger than a few files, and as a result, will not be using packages. However, Java provides many built-in packages, which we will make use of, using import statements.

Learning Objective #2
Import statements
let you use
other classes.

The next line is the import statement.

```
import java.io.*;
```

Import statements are very important in Java. They allow you to use classes from other packages. These packages may be packages you have created, or they may be Java system packages. In the case of the above import line, we are using a Java system package named "io". The * on the end specifies that we want to import all of the classes from io.

There are actually two ways you can import. You can import every class in a package, such as I just demonstrated. Or you can only import the classes you are going to actually use. If you examine the above program, you will see that we are using three classes: BufferedReader, InputStream, and IOException. We are also using System, but its automatically available without the need for an import. To import these three classes one by one, you would use the following lines of code:

```
import java.io.BufferedReader;
import java.io.InputStream;
import java.io.IOException;
```

Both of the two methods accomplish exactly the same thing; they will import the necessary classes. It is no less efficient to import all of the classes compared to just the classes you need. So which should you use? This is a controversial topic that has been the topic of debate among experienced Java programmers. Ultimately it just comes down to looks, and individual style. Some programmers think the single line looks better, some like seeing every class you use listed. This is the point at which a student in one of my face-to-face classes would always ask me, well Jeff, which do you prefer?

I will answer that, and I am sure I will get more than a few emails of disapproval. I have seen that as programs grow the number of import statements can get huge if you have each listed. It then becomes hard to maintain and its not really adding anything to the program. Because of this, I always use ".*" imports.

Single Line Comments

Comments are lines of code that do not affect how the program runs. Comments contain notes from the programmer, and can be in any format the programmer chooses. These notes make the program clearer and easier to understand. A single line comment can appear anywhere in source code and starts with //. A single line comment ends with the line. You can begin the next line with a single line comment as well. The following is an example of a single line comment.

Learning Objective #3
Comments help others (and you) know what your program is doing.

```
// this is a comment
```

If you wanted to, you could also create several lines of comments.

```
// Comment line 1
// Comment line 2
// Comment line 3
```

It is always a good idea to add comments to make your program source code easier to understand.

Single line comments can also coexist with regular code, on the same line. Consider the following line of code:

```
System.out.println("Hello"); // print out "Hello"
```

As you can see, the left side of the line is actual code, that will execute. The right side of the line, beginning with //, is a comment. Using a single line comment in this way can be useful to explain individual lines of code.

Multi Line Comments

You can also create a multi line comment. These comments can span for many lines and allows completely free-form text to be inserted into the comment. A multi line comment begins with /* and ends with */. The following shows an example of a multi line comment.

```
/*
Line 1
Line 2
Line 3
*/
```

Both single and multi line comments greatly add to the readability of your program – both for yourself and other programmers.

Class Declaration

Usually every Java source file defines one single class. Classes are the basic building block of Java programs. Very large applications may have hundreds, if not thousands, of classes. For now, you can think of a class as a program. Nearly every program in this book will consist of only one class. However, when we reach Chapter 13, you will learn how to create a program that has more than one class.

Classes are declared using the "class" statement. For example, the following class statement declares a class named UserInput.

```
public class UserInput
```

Inside of the classes are methods. These methods contain the actions to be carried out by the program. The most important method is the main method.

Learning Objective #4
The main method is where the program begins.

Main Method

The main method is where your program begins execution. The main method must be declared in a very strict format. The following shows how the main method should look.

```
public static void main(String args[])
{
// put main method actions here
}
```

Here you can see the main method being declared. The main method is public, so that everything can access it. Whenever you create a main method, which is once for every one of your Java applications, you should copy this main method header. There is little you can change about it. You will learn the exact meaning of the other parts of the main method when we study methods, in Chapter 6.

Semicolon and Curly Brace Usage

As you have been looking through these examples, it may be somewhat confusing as to when semicolons are used and when curly braces are used. You probably have also noticed that not all source code lines are left justi-fied. The program code is indented. These three topics will be discussed in this section.

Learning Objective #5
Use semicolons on lines that "end an idea".

Semicolon Usage

If you have never worked with a language that requires semicolon ter-minated lines, it can be a confusing idea. In Java, the semicolon ends an idea. So if you were going to print "Hello World", such as follows.

```
System.out.println("Hello World");
```

You would use a semicolon. The idea of this line has ended, it has done its job, and the next line is a new idea. However, consider an if-statement.

```
if(i<10)
{
  System.out.println("Hello");
}
```

The if-statement does NOT have a semicolon. The idea of the if-statement is not yet done, the lines that follow will only be executed if the if-statement is true.

Here is a very simple rule-of-thumb, which is almost always true. To determine if a line should have a semicolon, look at the next line. If the next line is an open curly brace then the line should NOT have a semicolon. There are exceptions to this rule, but it generally holds true.

The case where this rule does not work is when you begin to leave out curly braces as a shortcut. This is discussed in the next section.

When Curly Braces are not Needed

If there is just one line of code in an if-statement, while-loop, for-loop or do/while loop you can leave off the curly braces. For example consider the following if statement.

```
if( i<10 )
   System.out.println("i is less than 10");
else
   System.out.println("i is not less than 10");
```

Because there is only one line in the code block, the curly braces can be omitted. If you add another line of code to either block, that block must now use curly braces.

Indenting Code

You have probably noticed that the code examples that I give you are indented. This makes the source code much easier to read than if the entire file were left-justified. The rules for indenting are pretty simple. It is based on where curly braces are located, or could have been located. Consider the following program, which is indented, shown in Figure 3.1.

Figure 3.1: How indenting works

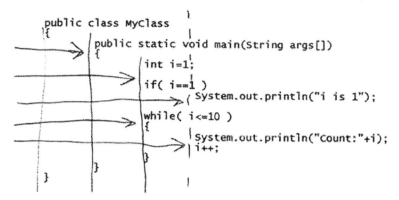

You will notice that there are four levels of indention. The first level is left justified and is denoted by my left most vertical line above. Then, each time there is an opening curly brace the indention level goes over by one. A closing curly brace will bring it back by one. Did you notice my dashed vertical line? The if-statement does not have a curly brace, but it could have. Because of this, we indent to the fourth level.

Variables

Variables are used to hold information while the program is processing it. Java uses nine variable types to hold different types of data. These nine types are summarized in Table 3.1.

Table 3.1: Java Variable Types

Learning Objective #6
Use the right
variable type for
the right purpose.

Data Type	Purpose
boolean	Used to store yes/no or true/false type information. Very common.
char	Used to store single char information. For example gender (i.e. 'm' or 'f'). Very common.
byte	Used to hold information that is normally represented as a byte of computer memory. Small values, less than 128.
short	Used to hold small numbers (<32,767) that require no decimal places.
int	Used to hold most numbers that do not require decimal places. Very common.
long	Used to hold very large numbers that do not require decimal places.
float	Used to hold numbers that require decimal places.
double	Used to hold large/precise numbers that require decimal places. Very common.
String	Used to hold non-numeric values, such as a person's name. Very common.

In normal programming practice you will use some of the variable data types much more often than others. The common data types are listed above. For now, you should focus primarily on the ones listed as very common.

Java data types can be broken into three groups, which all share similar characteristics.

- Numeric Data Types
- String Data Types
- Boolean Data Types

I will now explain each of these three groups, beginning with the numeric data types.

Numeric Data Types

Numeric data types are used to hold numbers. Within the numeric data types there are two subgroups:

- Integer Data Types
- Floating Point Data Types

Integer data types cannot have decimal places. If you try to assign a number, with decimal places, to an integer data type, the decimal places will drop off, no rounding will occur. Floating point data types can hold decimal places.

Java defines two integer data types: int and long. The only difference between int and long are the size of numbers they can hold. Usually you will use int, unless you need to hold a really large number. The sizes of all data types are summarized later in this section.

Java defines two floating point data types: float and double. The only difference between float and double are the size of numbers they can hold. Usually you will use double, as it can be handled most efficiently by Java. The sizes of all data types are summarized later in this section.

The following code block defines an int and assigned a value of 10 to the int.

```
int i;
i = 10;
```

The above code demonstrates how a variable of any data type can be defined. First, the data type, in this case int is specified. Secondly, the name of the variable, in this case "i" is specified. Finally, a semicolon ends the line. The above two lines can also be combined as follows:

```
int i - 10;
```

To print out a numeric data type use the println method, as follows:

```
System.out.println("The value of i is " + i );
```

Mathematical operations can easily be performed on numerical data types. The symbols + and - are used to add and subtract. The symbols / and * are used to multiply and divide. For example, to add five to "i" you would use the following code.

```
i = i + 1;
```

There are also two shortcut operators ++ and - - that both add and subtract one. For example, to increase "i" by one use the following code;

```
i++;
```

The shortcuts += and -= can also be used to add and subtract a number from a variable. For example, to increase "i" by five use the following code.

```
i+=5;
```

String Data Types

If you need to hold textual data you should use a string data type. For example, to create a String named str and assign it to the text "Java", you would use the following code.

```
String str;
str = "Java";
```

Just as with numeric data types these two steps can be combined as follows.

```
String str = "Java";
```

You can use the + operator with a string, just like numeric types, however, it has a different effect. Adding two strings attach, or concatenate, them together. For example, the following block of code would print out "HelloWorld".

```
String str = "Hello";
str = str + "World";
System.out.println(str);
```

The statement str = str + "World" attaches "World" to the end of str.

Important: You should only use a numeric data type when it makes sense to perform mathematical operations on the value (i.e. adding or subtracting from it). Otherwise, the data type used should be String. For example, a social security number should be a string because there is no value in adding or subtracting from a social security number.

Boolean Data Types

The final data type group is boolean. Boolean data types can hold only two values: true and false. A boolean is created much like any other variable in Java.

```
boolean done;
done = false;
```

Here a boolean named "done" is created and assigned to a value of false.

Data Type Sizes

Each numeric data type can hold a different sized number, the lengths of each datatype are summarized in Table 3.2.

Table 3.2: Numeric Datatype Sizes

Datatype	Signed	Range
char	n/a	16 bits
byte	yes	-128 to +127 (8 bits)
short	yes	-32,768 to +32,767
int	yes	-2,147,483,648 to 2,147,483,647 (32 bits)
long	yes	-9,223,372,036,854,775,808 to +9,223,372,036,854,775,807 (64 bits)
float	yes	Float.NEGATIVE_INFINITY to Float.POSITIVE_INFINITY (32 bits)
double	yes	Double.NEGATIVE_INFINITY to Double.POSITIVE_INFINITY (64 bits)

Java does not specify a maximum size for Strings, this is defined by your computer system. However, strings can become very large, if needed, up into the megabyte size range.

Important
You should only use a numeric data type when it makes sense to perform mathematical operations on the value.

Constants

You can also designate a variable as constant. A constant variable may not change its values. Constants are useful to define common numbers, such as pi. To create a constant variable put the keyword final in front of the variable. For example, the following line creates a pi constant.

```
final double pi = 3.14159265;
```

Data Type Conversion

Learning Objective #7
Know how to
convert data types.

Earlier in this chapter we saw how you can create both string and numeric data types. Often you will need to convert between the two. Consider an example where you have a string that contains 1001.

```
String str = "1001";
```

Now you would like to add 5 to the string. If you use the following line of code, you might not get what you expect.

```
str = str + 5;
```

What would str now contain? Would it contain "1006"? No it would not! It would actually contain "10015". This is because anything added to a string is concatenated. Which means it is simply tacked on to the end. To properly perform this operation you would have to convert str to an integer, perform the addition, then convert it back to a string. I will now show you how to perform this conversion. There are actually three conversion types that you will often do with numeric and string variables.

- Convert a string to a numeric
- Convert a numeric to string
- Convert a numeric to a different numeric

I will begin by showing you how to convert a string to a numeric.

Converting String to Numeric

Converting a string to a numeric is a very common operation to perform. Anytime you read data from the user it always is given to you in string form. No matter if you are using a console application or one of the more advanced GUI, data always comes in string form. Often, you will need to convert this user input into numeric form so that you can properly process the data. The following lines of code would convert our string, containing "1001" into an integer.

```
String str = "1001";
int i = Integer.parseInt(str);
```

By using the function "Integer.parseInt" you pass in str as an argument and the function returns an integer. Now that "i" contains an integer you can easily add 5 to it as follows.

```
i = i + 5;
```

The variable "i" will now contain 1006.

You may be wondering what would happen if you pass an invalid number into Integer.parseInt. For example, what would happen if you passed in the string "Java"? You might be able to guess the answer from the last section. What happens when a method or function is given data that it cannot handle? An exception is thrown! In this case, an exception named NumberFormatException is thrown. In the case of NumberFormatException, Java does NOT require us to catch it.

However, if you do not catch it, any invalid number that you might encounter is going to cause your program to crash. Because of this you should catch the NumberFormatException, especially if you are reading user input. You should NEVER assume that your user will give you valid data! The following code would prompt the user for a number and display an error if they provide an invalid number.

```
try
{
// display a prompt to the user
  System.out.print("Please enter a number>");

// create a stream to read from the user
  BufferedReader userInput = new BufferedReader(
```

```
                         new InputStreamReader(System.in));
```

Learning Objective #8
Know how to trap
an invalid number
exception.

```
// read a line of text from the user
  String str = userInput.readLine();

// attempt to convert the user's input into
// an integer
  int i = Integer.parseInt(str);
}
catch(IOException e)
{
  System.out.println("An IO exception occured.");
}
catch(NumberFormatException e)
{
  System.out.println("Enter a valid number!!");
}
```

The above block of code brings together several concepts we have learned. First a BufferedReader stream is created to read the string from the user. Next, a line of input is read from the user and converted to an int. Finally the user's input is converted into an integer.

Did you notice the catch blocks? There are two of them. Two catch blocks are required because two different exceptions can occur. First, the readLine function could throw an IOException. Secondly, the Integer.parseInt function could throw a NumberFormatException. When you have more than one exception type you are allowed to "stack" catch blocks like this.

Now that you have seen how to convert a string to an integer, you may be wondering about the other Java data types, such as short or double. You should be able to infer the correct function call from the data type. For example, to convert a double, you would use Double.parseDouble. Each of the function calls are summarized here.

- **byte**: Byte.parseByte(str)
- **double**: Double.parseDouble(str)
- **float**: Float.parseFloat(str)
- **int**: Integer.parseInt(str)
- **long**: Long.parseLong(str)
- **short**: Short.parseShort(str)

Important: The int type is inconsistent with the others. To convert to an int, you use Integer.parseInt, not Int.parseInt. Do not be confused by this, it is just an unfortunate inconsistency in the Java language.

Now that you have seen how to convert a string to a numeric, lets examine the opposite conversion.

Converting Numeric to String

Converting a numeric to a string is much easier than the reverse operation. You have already been converting numeric variables to strings, you just might not have been aware of it. Anytime you print out a variable with System.out.println, you are converting a numeric into a string.

```
int i - 1000;
System.out.println("The value of i is: " + i );
```

Here the value of "i" was converted to a string, attached to the end of the constant string and the result was printed out. So if you just want to convert to a string and not display the result, add to an empty constant string ("") and assign the result to a string.

```
int i = 1001;
String str = "" + i;
```

Now "i"" has been converted to a string named str. This will work just as well for all of the numeric data types.

Converting Numeric to Numeric

Sometimes you may want to convert one numeric type to another numeric type. So long as the target numeric type is larger than the source numeric type, this is okay. For example, assigning an int into a long is fine.

```
long l;
int i;

i = 10;
l = i;
```

Because a long is larger than an int, this is fine. You would not lose data making such a copy. However, if you try to copy a long into an int, you will run into a problem.

```java
long l;
int i;
l = 10;
i = l;
```

Now you will be given an error. You are trying to copy a long into an int. Of course we know that the number 10 would fit into the int just fine. However, Java makes no such distinction. If Java sees that the type on the left of an = is smaller than the type on the right, a compile error results.

If you really want to copy a long into an int you must tell Java that you really want to be doing this, and you do not mind that the result might not fit. You do this with a type-cast.

```java
long l;
int i;
l = 10;
i = (int)l;
```

Now you are converting the "l" variable into an int before it is assigned to "i". This will compile just fine. If you ever get an error converting from one numeric type to another just use a type-cast to convert the right side of the = to the correct type.

This same technique works on floating point numbers. You can also use it to strip the decimal places from a floating point number. For example, the following code would strip the decimal places from the double variable d.

```java
double d;
d = 10.5;
d = (double)((int)d);
System.out.println("The value of d is " + d );
```

The above code would display 10. Do you see how this is happening? First the double variable d is converted to an int. This conversion causes d to lose all decimal places. The result is truncated, not rounded. But then, the result is converted back into a double, so that it can be assigned back into d.

Chapter Review

In this chapter you learned about how a Java program is structured. You learned what the major parts of the Java source files are for. You were also introduced to variables. Variables allow the program to hold values while it processes data. Variables are very important to programming, and it is very important that you understand how they work.

You learned the difference between strings and numbers. You saw that strings hold text data and numbers can perform mathematical operations. You can also convert between Strings and numbers. Java supports many different types of variables. Some can hold bigger numbers than others.

You learned about comments and how they can make your program easier to understand. Java supports both single-line and multi-line comments. Single line comments begin with a //. Multi line comments are between a beginning /* and an ending */.

New Terms

boolean A primitive datatype that holds true or false.

Boolean class A holder class for the boolean primitive datatype.

char A primitive data type that holds single characters. To hold multiple characters, see the String class.

Comment A note that is placed in the program by the programmer. The comment has no effect on the way that the program runs. Comments can be single line or multi-line.

byte A Java primitive data type that holds very small numbers that would fit into a single byte.

Byte class A holder class for the byte primitive datatype.

Constant A variable that holds a fixed value and cannot be changed. Java constants always start with the keyword final.

double A Java primitive datatype that can hold floating point numbers. The double datatype is larger than the float datatype.

Double class A holder class for the double primitive datatype.

final The Java keyword that designates a variable as constant.

float A Java primitive data type that holds floating point numbers. The float datatype is smaller than the double datatype.

Float class A holder class for the float primitive datatype.

indent Java source code is indented to make it appear clearer.

int A Java primitive datatype used to hold numbers. The int datatype is smaller than the long datatype, but larger than the short datatype.

Integer class A holder class for the integer primitive datatype.

long A Java primitive datatype used to hold numbers. The long datatype is larger than the int datatype.

Long class A holder class for the long primitive datatype.

Primitive Data Type A datatype that is not a class. Java's primitive datatypes are: char, byte, short, int, long, float, double and boolean.

short A Java primitive datatype that holds numbers. The short datatype is smaller than the int datatype.

Short class A holder class for the short primitive datatype.

String A Java class that can hold text data.

Type Cast To convert from one datatype to another. A cast is usually denoted by the desired datatype in parenthesis, such as (int).

Review Questions

1. What is the primary difference between double and long?

2. What datatype would you use to store the number of students in a class?

3. What datatype would you use to store someone's hourly wage (i.e. $12.50)?

4. Is String a primitive data type? Why or why not?

5. What is the purpose of the final keyword?

Assignment #3

You must correct the following program. This program is attempting to add the numbers "2" and "3", but it is currently displaying "23". It should display "5". Correct the program so that the numbers "2" and "3" are properly converted before they are added.

public class Assignment3

```
{
  public static void main(String args[])
  {
    String str1 = "1";
    String str2 = "2";

    System.out.println("Result:" + (str1+str2) );
  }
}
```

CHAPTER 4: HANDLING USER INPUT

In Chapter 4 you will learn about:
- **Reading from the User**
- **Reading Strings**
- **Reading Numbers**
- **Error Handling**

The programs that we have looked at so far do not prompt the user for any information. The program simply executes to completion and then quits. Now I will show you how to create an application that is able to prompt the user for information, and process that information.

There are many different ways that input can be gathered from the user. The most common two methods are the keyboard and mouse. In this chapter we will learn how to receive input from the user, using the keyboard. The user will be allowed to enter a line of text, right on the console window. This line of text will be returned to the Java program for processing.

How to Read Data from the User

I will begin by showing you a simple program that will read data from the user. This program will only read the data from the user in text form. If you want to read data from the user in numeric form, you will have to first read the data as a string, and then convert it to numeric form. This technique will be discussed later in this chapter.

However, before we see how to input numbers, we will start with inputting strings. Inputting a string in Java is not as straightforward as you might think. Java provides no direct command to prompt for a line of text from the user. Because of this, some extra setup must be done, on our part, to enable Java to read lines of text from the user.

Java does not require too much additional code to read from the user. This additional code is the same for each program you write, so you will be able to copy the code, presented in Listing 4.1, to any program that needs to read lines of text from the console.

I will now show you an example program that reads lines of text from the user. This program will demonstrate what needs to be added to a Java program to read lines of text from the user. First, we will examine a simple program that prompts the user for their name, and then says "Hello" to that user. Listing 4.1 shows this program.

Listing 4.1: Read Data from the User (Hello.java)

```java
import java.io.*;

public class Hello
{
  public static void main(String args[])
  {
    try
    {
      InputStreamReader inputStreamReader =
        new InputStreamReader ( System.in );
      BufferedReader in =
        new BufferedReader ( inputStreamReader );
      System.out.print("What is your name? ");
      String name = in.readLine();
      System.out.println("Hello " + name );
    }
    catch(IOException e)
    {
    }
  }
}
```

Learning Objective #1
Read strings
from the user.

You will notice that it takes quite a few extra lines to actually accept input from the user. Most of them you do not need to be directly concerned with how they work. The line that actually reads the input is the first line below:

```java
String name = in.readLine();
System.out.println("Hello " + name );
```

The above lines wait for a user to enter something and then press enter. What ever string the user enters will be placed into the string named "name". Then, after the user enters their name, the program displays the word "Hello" followed by the user's name.

Additional Lines Needed

In addition to the two lines just discussed, there are quite a few additional lines of program code that are necessary to make this program work. While these lines do not directly interact with the user, they are quite necessary. I will now show you what they are for, so that you can include them in your own programs.

Try and Catch Blocks

If you look at Listing 4.1 you will see that there is a try and catch block. Try/catch blocks are used to handle errors. If any error occurs in the middle of the try block, the program immediately executes the catch block. If no error occurs, the catch block will not be executed.

The general form of a try/catch block is shown here.

```
try
{
  // program code that may cause an error
}
catch(Exception e)
{
  // program code to be executed if an error occurs
}
```

If you are going to have a catch block, you must have a try block. It makes no sense for them to exist separately. If an error occurs anywhere within the try block, the program will immediately leave the try block and execute the code in the catch block.

This allows the program to continue executing, even though an error has occurred. Usually, you will insert some code to display an error message to the user when the catch block is executed.

You may be wondering, what error could possibly happen while reading data from the keyboard. In reality, there is no error that can occur. However, because readLine is a part of the Input/Output system of Java, you must register to handle the error, even though it cannot actually happen.

Setting up to Read User Input

In addition to the try/catch block, you must also setup a few objects to allow your program to read from the user. These objects are created by using the following two lines:

Reusable Code
These lines can be added to any program that needs to read from the user.

```
InputStreamReader inputStreamReader =
  new InputStreamReader ( System.in );
BufferedReader in =
  new BufferedReader ( inputStreamReader );
```

These lines deal with Java's Input/Output system and allow you to read data from the user line by line. It is not important that you understand how these two lines work. You simply need to be aware that they must be included in any program that needs to read user input from the console keyboard.

Once you have executed these two lines you will be left with an object named "in". This object is used to call the readLine method.

Reading Numbers

In the last example you saw how to read a string. Now I will show you how to read a number. It is necessary to read a number if you want to perform any sort of mathematical operation on what the user has entered.

Learning Objective #2
Read numbers
from the user.

Probably the easiest way to read a number is to first read a String, and then convert it to a number. Java provides several methods to convert from a string to a numeric type. Which method you use depends on the type of number you want.

- **byte**: Byte.parseByte(str)
- **double**: Double.parseDouble(str)
- **float**: Float.parseFloat(str)
- **int**: Integer.parseInt(str)
- **long**: Long.parseLong(str)
- **short**: Short.parseShort(str)

For this example we will input a number, in miles, and convert that number into kilometers. Listing 4.2 shows this example program.

Listing 4.2: Input Numbers (InputNumbers.java)

```java
import java.io.*;

public class InputNumbers
{
  public static void main(String args[])
  {
    try
    {
      InputStreamReader inputStreamReader =
        new InputStreamReader ( System.in );
      BufferedReader in =
        new BufferedReader ( inputStreamReader );
      System.out.print("Enter a length in miles? ");
```

```
      String miles = in.readLine();
      double dMiles = Double.parseDouble(miles);
      double dKilometers = 1.609344 *dMiles;
      System.out.println("That is " + dKilometers +
        " kilometers.");
    }
    catch(IOException e)
    {
    }
  }
}
```

As you can see from the above program it is very similar to the previous example where a string was entered into the program.

However, once the string has been read into the variable "miles", the string is converted into a double. The string is converted into a double, rather than an long, because doubles can have decimal places.

To convert the string into a double, the following line of code is used.

```
double dMiles = Double.parseDouble(miles);
```

To convert the number of miles into Kilometers the miles are multiplied by 1.609344. You may want to define a constant, using the final keyword, to hold this number.

Handling Bad Numbers

We now have a useful program to convert miles into Kilometers. However, the program has one fatal flaw. What happens if you enter an invalid number into it? What happens if you enter something such as "one1one", or some other nonsense string. Try it and see.

If you enter a non-valid number your program will crash with a NumberFormatException.

Learning Objective #3
Handling bad numbers, without crashing the program.

You do not want your program to behave in this way. A properly designed program should never throw an exception and crash.

To keep from crashing as a result of a bad number, you must add an additional catch block to your program to handle the NumberFormatException. Listing 4.3 shows how to do this.

Listing 4.3: Handle Bad Numbers (BadNumbers.java)

```java
import java.io.*;

public class BadNumbers
{
  public static void main(String args[])
  {
    try
    {
      InputStreamReader inputStreamReader =
        new InputStreamReader ( System.in );
      BufferedReader in =
        new BufferedReader ( inputStreamReader );
      System.out.print("Enter a length in miles? ");
      String miles = in.readLine();
      double dMiles = Double.parseDouble(miles);
      double dKilometers = 1.609344 *dMiles;
      System.out.println("That is " + dKilometers +
        " kilometers.");
    }
    catch(NumberFormatException e)
    {
      System.out.println(
        "You entered an invalid number.");
    }
    catch(IOException e)
    {
    }
  }
}
```

The above program is nearly the same as the last example, except that four additional lines are added. These four lines will handle the exception, caused by an invalid number.

```java
catch(NumberFormatException e)
{
  System.out.println(
    "You entered an invalid number.");
}
```

The above catch block will handle any exception of the type NumberFormatException. The parseDouble method will throw this type of exception if it is passed an invalid number. By adding this catch block, your program is able to display an error, rather than crashing.

Very Important! In this example, we already had a catch block. But we needed to add a new catch block for a new exception type. You can add as many catch blocks onto a try block as you need. Add one catch block for every type of exception that you need to handle.

Displaying Data

We have seen that there are two different ways to display data to the console window. The following two methods both display data to the console window.

```
System.out.print
System.out.println
```

But what exactly is the difference between these two methods? First, we will look at what System.out.println does. Consider the following two lines of code.

```
System.out.println("Hello");
System.out.println("World");
```

These two lines would produce the following output.

```
Hello
World
```

Learning Objective #4
Know the difference between println and print.

Now consider if we were to use print instead of println. Consider the following two lines of code that use print.

```
System.out.print("Hello");
System.out.print("World");
```

If you executed the above two lines of code you would get a different output. These two lines of code would produce the following output.

```
HelloWorld
```

As you can see, System.out.println moves to a new line. Whereas System.out.print does not move to a new line.

Chapter Review

In this chapter you learned how to read input from the user. All input from the user is read initially as a string. If you need to read data from the user in other formats, you must first read the data as a string, and then convert it to the appropriate type. Java provides many different methods to convert strings into other data types.

You also learned about try/catch blocks. Try/catch blocks are used to handle errors in Java programs. The try block is used to enclose code that you suspect may throw an exception. If an exception is thrown in code that is not inside of a try block, your program will crash. A properly designed program should never crash. If an error is detected by the try block, the program will immediately execute the catch.

New Terms

BufferedStreamReader A Java class that is used to read data from a device. For this book, it is used only to read data from the keyboard.

catch The catch-block allows the Java program to handle its own errors, and not simply terminate when an exception happens. When an exception occurs inside of a try-block, the code inside of the catch-block is executed to handle that error.

crash When a program stops in an unplanned manor. Usually the crash is the result of an exception that was not caught.

Exception An exception occurs in Java when an error occurs. Exceptions, if not caught, will cause the program to crash.

InputStreamReader A Java class that is used to read data from a device. For this book, it is used only to read data from the keyboard.

NumberFormatException An exception that occurs when a non-number string is passed to one of the parse functions. For example, the string "182g" would produce this exception if used with Integer.parseInt.

Numeric Datatype A datatype that holds numbers, and can have mathematical operations performed on it.

print A Java method that will display a line of text, but not move to the next line.

println A Java method that will display a line of text, and will move to the next line.

readLine A Java method that prompts the user to enter a line of text. The user is allowed to enter text until the user presses the ENTER key.

String Datatype A datatype that holds text information. You cannot preform mathematical operations on the String.

System A Java class that provides many important methods and variables for interacting with the computer system.

System.in The standard input. This variable is used to receive keyboard input from the user.

System.out The standard output. This variable is used to display data on the console.

try The try block encloses code that might cause an exception. If an exception does happen in a try block, the try block's catch block executes.

Review Questions

1. How do you read a number from the user?

2. What is the difference between print and println?

3. What happens if a "bad number" is passed to a method such as Integer. parseInt?

4. How do you handle "bad numbers" properly in a Java program?

5. What is the purpose of a try/catch block?

Assignment #4

Write a program that will accept a number of miles from the user. This value should accept decimal places (i.e. 1.5 miles). Convert the number of miles into kilometers. Display the number of kilometers with decimal places (i.e. 3.445 kilometers). You do not have to round, display as many decimal places as Java gives you.

Note: 1 mile = 1.609344 kilometers.

CHAPTER 5: MAKING DECISIONS

In Chapter 5 you will learn about:
- Comparing Values
- If/Else Statements
- And/Or
- Switch/Case

So far we have only accepted data from the user and displayed that data. Sometimes the data was processed slightly before being redisplayed, but no decisions were made based on that data. In this chapter you will see how your program can make decisions based on the data that the user enters.

Comparing Values

For your program to make decisions, it must compare values. In this chapter I will show you how to compare different types of values.

Comparing a Numeric Value

First I will show you how to compare a variable to a numeric value. This is done by simply using ==. For example, if you wanted to compare the variable "i", you could use the following lines of code.

```
int i=5;
if( i==5 )
{
   System.out.println("i contains the value 5");
}
```

Very important! Notice how I used the == to compare the value of "i". This is how you compare values in Java. A single = means assign the value, such as:

```
i=5;
```

The above statement will assign the value of 5 to i. Do not confuse the assignment (=) with the comparison (==).

Learning Objective #1
Learn to compare numeric values.

Important
Always compare numbers with double equal (==), not single equal (=).

Now lets look at a complete example. Listing 5.1 shows a program that compares to see if a variable is above a certain number or not.

Listing 5.1: Are You Old Enough (OldEnough.java)

```java
import java.io.*;

class OldEnough
{
  public static void main(String args[])
  {
    try
    {
      InputStreamReader inputStreamReader =
        new InputStreamReader ( System.in );
      BufferedReader in =
        new BufferedReader ( inputStreamReader );
      System.out.print("How old are you? ");
      String age = in.readLine();
      int iAge = Integer.parseInt(age);
      if( iAge>=18 )
      {
        System.out.println(
"You are old enough to vote in the United States.");
      }
      if( iAge<18 )
      {
        System.out.println(
          "You are not old enough to vote in" +
          " the United States");
      }
    }
    catch(NumberFormatException e)
    {
      System.out.println("That is not a valid age.");
    }
    catch(IOException e)
    {
    }
  }
}
```

This program will prompt the user to see how old they are. If the user is 18 or over, the user will be informed that they are old enough to vote in the United States. If the user is below 18 years, the user will be informed that they are not old enough to vote in the United States.

This program does this by using the "if statement" to check the age of the user.

```
if( iAge>=18 )
{
  System.out.println(
"You are old enough to vote in the United States.");
}
```

Notice the if statement. It names the variable to compare and what to compare it against. Here we are checking to see if the variable "iAge" is greater than, or equal to, the value 18.

Comparing a String Value

Comparing a string is somewhat different than comparing a number. You may be tempted to use == to compare a string. This will not work properly, even though it will compile correctly. Consider Listing 5.2.

Listing 5.2: Compare a String (InvalidString.java)

```
import java.io.*;

class InvalidString
{
  public static void main(String args[])
  {
    try
    {
      InputStreamReader inputStreamReader =
        new InputStreamReader ( System.in );
      BufferedReader in =
        new BufferedReader ( inputStreamReader );
      System.out.print(
        "What is your favorite color? ");

      String color = in.readLine();

      if( color=="red" )
        System.out.println(
          "My favorite color is red too!");
```

Learning Objective #2
Learn to compare two strings, always use .equals, not ==.

WRONG!!!
This is wrong! Never use == to compare two strings.

```
      }
      catch(IOException e)
      {
      }
    }
  }
}
```

This example program will not work. It does not properly compare two strings. This is a very confusing aspect of Java, but unfortunately you cannot use the double equal (==) to compare two strings. Using == asks Java if the two strings occupy the same location in memory. Normally you really don't care if two strings are at the same location in memory, so using == with strings is unsuitable.

To properly compare two strings you must use the "equals" method of the String class. Listing 5.3 shows the same program that we just examined, only using the "equals" method.

Listing 5.3: Check for a Valid String (ValidString.java)

Correct!

Always use ".equals" to compare two strings.

```
import java.io.*;

class ValidString
{
  public static void main(String args[])
  {
    try
    {
      InputStreamReader inputStreamReader =
        new InputStreamReader ( System.in );
      BufferedReader in =
        new BufferedReader ( inputStreamReader );

      System.out.print(
        "What is your favorite color? ");

      String color = in.readLine();

      if( color.equals("red") )
        System.out.println(
          "My favorite color is red too!");

    }
    catch(IOException e)
    {
    }
  }
}
```

The Else Statement

The "else" statement can be combined with the "if" statement. The "else" statement specifies what to do if the "if" statement is not true. If you create an if/else block, then you are guaranteed that at least one part of it will execute. If the "if" part is true, it will be executed. If the "if" part is not true, then the "else" part will be executed. The general format of an if/else statement is as follows.

```
if( a==1 )
{
  // this part will be executed if a is 1
}
else
{
  // this part will be executed if a is not 1
}
```

Learning Objective #3
Learn to use the
if/else combination.

Now lets look at an example that uses an if/else statement. Listing 5.4 shows a modified version of the favorite color program we just examined. Listing 5.4 shows an example of using else.

Listing 5.4: Else Example (StringElse.java)

```
import java.io.*;

class StringElse
{
  public static void main(String args[])
  {
    try
    {
      InputStreamReader inputStreamReader =
        new InputStreamReader ( System.in );
      BufferedReader in =
        new BufferedReader ( inputStreamReader );
      System.out.print(
        "What is your favorite color? ");

      String color = in.readLine();

      if( color.equals("red") )
      {
        System.out.println(
```

```
                    "My favorite color is red too!");
        }
        else
        {
          System.out.println("I guess " + color +
            " is okay, but I like red better.");
        }

      }
      catch(IOException e)
      {
      }
    }
}
```

This program will prompt the user for their favorite color. If the user chooses "red" as their favorite color, the program will agree with them. Otherwise the program will state that the user's color is okay, but it prefers red. This is done with the else statement.

If/Else Ladders

As you saw in the last section you can connect "if" statements with "else" statements. You can connect these into long ladders. This allows you to process several different options. Listing 5.5 shows an if/else ladder.

Listing 5.5: If/Else Ladder (NumberIf.java)

```java
import java.io.*;

class NumberIf
{
  public static void main(String args[])
  {
    try
    {
      InputStreamReader inputStreamReader =
        new InputStreamReader ( System.in );
      BufferedReader in =
        new BufferedReader ( inputStreamReader );
      System.out.print(
        "Enter a number between 1 and 5? ");
      String num = in.readLine();
      int number = Integer.parseInt(num);

      if( number==1 )
      {
```

```
      System.out.println("You entered One.");
    }
    else if( number==2 )
    {
      System.out.println("You entered Two.");
    }
    else if( number==3 )
    {
      System.out.println("You entered Three.");
    }
    else if( number==4 )
    {
      System.out.println("You entered Four.");
    }
    else if( number==5 )
    {
      System.out.println("You entered Five.");
    }
    else
    {
      System.out.println(
      "You did not enter a number between 1 and 5.");
    }
  }
  catch(NumberFormatException e)
  {
    System.out.println(
      "You must enter a valid number.");
  }
  catch(IOException e)
  {
  }
  }
}
```

This program asks you to enter a number. For numbers 1-5 it will print out the word form of the number. For example it will print out "one" if you enter "1". This is done with an if/else ladder.

Using Logical AND and OR

You can create "compound if statements" that make even more intelligent decisions, using AND and OR. First we will look at how to use AND. In Java, logical AND is represented by &&.

Using If Statements with AND

First, we will consider if statements that make use of AND. For example, say you wanted to create an if statement that would only process if x were in the range between 10 and 100. You could do this with an if-statement using an AND. The following if-statement would do this.

```
if( (x>=10) && (x<=100) )
{
   System.out.println(" x is between 10 and 100");
}
```

The above if-statement would be read "if x is greater than or equal to 10 and x is less than or equal to 100", do this.

For the AND statement to be true, both sides must be true. Table 5.1 summarizes the AND statement.

Table 5.1: Truth Table for x && y (AND)

x	y	x && y
false	false	false
false	true	false
true	false	false
true	true	true

Using If Statements with OR

Now we will consider if statements that make use of OR. For example, say you wanted to create an if statement that would only process if x were equal to 10 or 100. You could do this with an if-statement using an OR. The following if-statement would do this.

```
if( (x==10) || (x==100) )
{
   System.out.println(" x is either 10 or 100");
}
```

The above if-statement would be read "if x is equal to 10 or x is equal to 100", do this.

For the OR statement to be true, both one-side must be true. Table 5.2 summarizes the OR statement.

Table 5.2: Truth Table for x || y (OR)

x	y	x ‖ y
false	false	false
false	true	true
true	false	true
true	true	true

By using both AND and OR you can create if statements that make more complex decisions.

Using the Switch/Case Statement

You can also use switch/case statements in place of the if/else ladder. Switch/case statements only work with integers, they do not work with strings. So if you want to compare a string, you will have to use an if/else ladder.

A switch/case contains a switch statement with many cases inside of it. Each case specifies what should be done when the case statement's number is passed to the switch statement. Finally a default, at the end, specifies what to do if none of the cases matched.

Listing 5.6 shows the number program, from the last section, rewritten as a switch/case program.

Important
Switch/case will not work with strings or floating point.

Listing 5.6: Using Switch/Case (NumberCase.java)

```
import java.io.*;

class NumberCase
{
  public static void main(String args[])
  {
    try
    {
      InputStreamReader inputStreamReader =
        new InputStreamReader ( System.in );
      BufferedReader in =
        new BufferedReader ( inputStreamReader );
      System.out.print(
        "Enter a number between 1 and 5? ");
      String num = in.readLine();
      int number = Integer.parseInt(num);

      switch( number )
      {
```

Learning Objective #5
Learn to use switch/case.

```
                    case 1:
                      System.out.println("You entered One.");
                      break;
                    case 2:
                      System.out.println("You entered Two.");
                      break;
                    case 3:
                      System.out.println("You entered Three.");
                      break;
                    case 4:
                      System.out.println("You entered Four.");
                      break;
                    case 5:
                      System.out.println("You entered Five.");
                      break;
                    default:
                      System.out.println(
              "You did not enter a number between 1 and 5.");
                      break;
                  }
                }
                catch(NumberFormatException e)
                {
                  System.out.println(
                    "You must enter a valid number.");
                }
                catch(IOException e)
                {
                }
              }
            }
```

Important

Make sure to end each case statement with a break, or it will execute the next case statement as well.

As you **can see** there is a case for each of the numbers to be compared. At the **end there is a** default that specifies what to do if none of the cases match.

Very important! Notice how each of the cases ends with a "break" statement? This is required to cause your program to exit the switch block. If you leave out the break, the program will begin executing the next case, and keep on going, until it hits a break.

Chapter Review

In this chapter we saw how programs can make decisions. You saw that programs use "if statements" to make decisions. An "if statement" allows the program to check the value of something and perform a task, if the value is what is expected.

You can also use "else" statements in conjunction with "if" statements. These "else" statements specify an action to take if the "if" statement failed to execute. Using these "else" statements, you can create long if/else ladders. These ladders allow your program to do many comparisons in a row.

If you are comparing a numeric value you can use a switch/case in place of the if/else ladder. It is important to remember that switch/case statements cannot be used on strings. If you want to compare a string to many different values, you must use an if/else ladder. You can also place a "default" statement at the end of the switch/case. The "default" statement will be executed if none of the cases match.

New Terms

case A case statement occurs inside of a switch statement. There is one case statement for each decision that the switch/case can make.

default If none of the case statements are executed, and a default statement is provided, the default statement will be executed.

else The else statement works with the if statement. If the if statement does not execute, then the else statement will be executed.

equals The equals method can be used to compare two strings. For example str.equals("Java") compares str to "Java".

equalsIgnoreCase The equalsIgnoreCase method can be used to compare two strings, without regard to case. For example str.equalsIgnoreCase("Java") compares str to "JAVA" would be true.

if The if statement allows Java to make decisions and compare variables.

if/else Ladder A series of if/else statements together is called an if/else ladder. If/else laddres are often replaced with switch/case statements.

switch Switch statements are used to compare a variable to any of the provided case statements. If no case statement matches, the default statement (if provided) will be executed.

Review Questions

1. What are if/else ladders often replaced with?

2. If no case statement matches what happens?

3. How do you compare two strings in Java?

4. Is it possible to make it through an if/else statement and execute neither the if or else body?

5. How do you use a switch/case with a String?

Assignment #5

Write a program that will input three things about the user.

- The user's name
- The user's age
- The user's country of citizenship

You must now determine if the user is eligible to vote in your country. If the user is, then notify them, using their name, that they are old enough to vote.

Note: For the United States, check to see if the user enters USA as the country of citizenship, and the age is 18 or greater. If it is, then notify the user that they are old enough to vote. For example, if the user enters USA, a name of "Jeff" and 21, the program would respond.

```
Hello Jeff, you are eligible to vote in the USA.
```

If I had entered Jeff, 21 and the United Kingdom, the program would respond:

```
Hello Jeff, you are not eligible to vote in the United
States.
```

Of course, if you are using a country other than the USA, your output will follow that countries voting age requirements.

CHAPTER 6: METHODS AND FUNCTIONS

In Chapter 6 you will learn about:
- **Variable Scope**
- **Functions**
- **Methods**
- **By Reference/By Value**
- **Instance Variables**
- **Variable Scope**

In the Chapter 3 we learned about variables. You saw that there were different variable data types. There are also different variable scope types. But what exactly is scope? Variable scope refers to what can access a variable and what cannot access a variable. There are three levels of scope for variables in Java.

- Static Variables
- Instance Variables
- Local Variables

You will find that you commonly use all three types of variable scope types. It is important to understand the difference between them. In this section I will show you how all three variable types work. I will begin with static variables.

Static Variables

Static variables always retain their values. Static local variables will hold their values between method or function calls. Static class-level variables will hold their values across all instances of a class. First I will show you an example of a static local variable. Listing 6.1 shows using a local variable.

Learning Objective #1
Understand static variables.

Listing 6.1: Using a Static Variable (MyClassStatic.java)

```java
public class MyClassStatic
{
  static int x = 0;

  public static void myMethod()
  {
    System.out.println( "Value of x:" + x );
```

```
    x++;
  }

  public static void main(String args[])
  {
    myMethod();
    myMethod();
    myMethod();
  }
}
```

If you were to run this program the output would be the numbers 0,1 and 2 all on separate lines. The keyword static in front of the local variable x is causing it to hold its value between method calls. This is not normal behavior for local variables, as you will see later in this section.

Static variables can also be class level, as the following example shows. Listing 6.2 shows an example of using a class level static variable.

Listing 6.2: Using a Static Class Variable (MyClassLevelStatic.java)

```
public class MyClassLevelStatic
{
  static int x = 0;

  public static void myMethod()
  {
    System.out.println( "Value of x:" + x );
    x++;
  }

  public static void main(String args[])
  {
    x = 10;
    myMethod();
    myMethod();
    myMethod();
  }
}
```

If you were to run the above program the output would be 10,11 and 12 all on separate lines. The variable x is declared outside of any method or function, because of this, it is class level and can be accessed from anywhere in the class. The variable is also static, so it can be accessed from both static and nonstatic methods. When x is assigned to 10 in the main method, that x is the same x that is increased by myMethod.

Instance Variables

Instance variables are declared outside of a function or method. Instance variables can be accessed anywhere in the class in which they were declared. A new set of instance variables is created for each class instance created. Consider the following example in Listing 6.3.

Listing 6.3: Using an Instance Variable (MyClassInstance.java)

```
class MyClassInstance
{
  public int x = 0;

  public static void main(String args[])
  {
    MyClassInstance myclass1 = new MyClassInstance();
    MyClassInstance myclass2 = new MyClassInstance();

    myclass1.x = 10;
    myclass2.x = 15;

    System.out.println(
      "Current value of myclass1.x is ",myclass1.x);
  }
}
```

This program will print out 10. There are two instances of MyClass created, named myclass1 and myclass2. Each of these two instances have their own copy of the instance variables, and as a result each have their own unique x variable. If x were to have been declared static, they would have been the same variable. A static x would have caused 15 to be printed out.

Local Variables

Local variables are declared inside of a method. These local variables can only be accessed from within the method. Unless the local variable is declared static, the local variable will lose its value when the method returns. When programming Java, most of the time you will create nonstatic local variables, like I am about to show you. Listing 6.4 shows local variables.

Learning Objective #2
Understand local variables.

Listing 6.4: Using an Instance Variable (MyClassLocal.java)

```
public class MyClassLocal
{
  public static void myMethod()
  {
    int x = 0;
    System.out.println( "Value of x:" + x );
```

```
    x++;
  }

  public static void main(String args[])
  {
    myMethod();
    myMethod();
    myMethod();
  }
}
```

This program would display the number 0 three times. The variable x is local. Each time the method is called x is reset to zero. As you can see this is very different from the static local variable used earlier in this section.

Functions and Methods

You have already seen functions and methods in previous chapters. Instead of using existing functions and methods, now we will now focus on how to create your own functions and methods. You may have already heard of functions and methods from other programming languages. Java methods are often known by different names in other programming languages. Some programming languages will refer to methods as subroutines, functions or sub-programs.

Regardless of what term methods go by their role is the same. A method or function allows you to take a commonly used piece of code and reuse it. If you are writing a program to manage an address book you will likely need to sort data at some point. You would likely isolate the sorting logic in a single method named "sort". Methods and functions are nearly the same. The only difference between a function and a method is:

- Methods do not return a value
- Functions do return a value

Create Your Own Function

First lets see what a function looks like. The following function accepts two integers and returns an integer. The return value will be the greater of the two integers passed in.

```
public static int max(int x,int y)
{
  if( x>y )
    return x;
  else
    return y;
}
```

Consider the following sections of the above method. They are summarized in Table 6.1.

Table 6.1: Sections of a Method

The return type:	int
The parameters:	x & y, both int's
Returns:	The two return statements
The modifiers:	static and public

Calling the above method would be very easy. To assign the variable "i" to the maximum of 10 and 100, you would do the following.

```
int i = max(10,100);
```

A function without a return type is called a method. Consider the following method.

```
public static void printName()
{
   System.out.println("Java");
}
```

It looks just like a function except the return type is void, which means no return type.

Your Own Static Methods

Using static on a method or function causes it to operate at the class level. Normally a method operates at the instance, or object, level. If you have not worked with object oriented design, understanding the difference between instance and class level may be somewhat confusing. First, make sure you know the difference between a class and an object.

Table 6.2: The Difference Between a Class and an Object

Learning Objective #4
Understand the
difference between a
class and an object.

Class	A class is a type of something, you do not use the class directly. (i.e. Toyota™ Rav4™) A class name usually starts with an uppercase letter.
Object	An object is one instance of a class. (i.e. my blue Toyota™ Rav4™) A object name usually starts with a lowercase letter.

Class
A class is a "type of" something.

Object
An object is an instance of a class.

Most of the methods and functions that we have examined this far have always been static. But what exactly does static method or function mean? First lets examine a program that makes use of a static function. The following program has one method that will return the value passed to it multiplied by ten. This class creates a method named multiply. Notice that the multiply method is static, just like the main method. This means that the main method can call the multiply function without having to instantiate the MyClass class. Listing 6.5 shows a static method.

Listing 6.5: Using a Static Function (MyClassStaticFunction.java)

```
public class MyClassStaticFunction
{
  public static int multiply(int i)
  {
    return(i*5);
  }

  public static void main(String args[])
  {
    int j = 5;
    j = multiply(j);
    System.out.println(j);
  }
}
```

Because multiply is declared static you do not need to use new to create a new instance of the class. You can simply access the multiply method directly from the main method. While this does make it easier to call a method, it prevents the method from using any instance variables. Static methods may not access nonstatic instance variables. This is a fairly big limitation, and as a result most methods are declared nonstatic.

Your Own Nonstatic Methods

Most of the functions and methods that you will create as a Java programmer will not be static. Static methods and functions cannot access instance variables, therefore, sometimes it is best to instantiate the class, and then use it by calling a nonstatic method. Listing 6.6 instantiates and uses a nonstatic method.

Listing 6.6: Using a Nonstatic Method (MyClassNonStaticMethod.java)

```java
public class MyClassNonStaticMethod
{
  public int total; // instance variable

  public void add(int i)
  {
    total = total + i;
  }

  public static void main(String args[])
  {
    MyClassNonStaticMethod myObject =
      new MyClassNonStaticMethod();
    MyClassNonStaticMethod myOtherObject =
      new MyClassNonStaticMethod();

    myObject.add(5);
    myOtherObject.add(3);
    myObject.add(10);
    myObject.add(10);

    System.out.println("Total myObject is:" +
      myObject.total );
    System.out.println("Total myOtherObject is:" +
      myOtherObject.total );
  }
}
```

As you can see, there are two object instances created: myObject and myOtherObject. This causes two separate instances of the total instance variable to be kept. The add methods, when called will add the number to their object's instance of x. As a result this program prints out 15 and 13.

Using Static Classes

Java contains a very useful class named Math. We have already used the Math class to obtain random numbers. What is very unique about the Math class is that every method is static. It is illegal to instantiate the Math class. For example, the following program is incorrect.

Important: DON'T DO THIS! It is illegal to instantiate the Math class.

```
public static void main(String args[])
{
  Math m = new Math(); // Never do this!
  System.out.println(m.max(1,2));
}
```

If you would like to use the max method of Math, simply call it directly.

```
public static void main(String args[])
{
  System.out.println(Math.max(1,2));
}
```

As you can see the max function is called directly from the Math class. This sort of call can be made on static functions/methods.

How Arguments are Passed

If you have worked with other programming languages you have likely heard of passing variables "by reference" or "by value". If you are not familiar with these terms, the meaning refers to what happens to the value of a method or function's arguments when that function ends. Consider Listing 6.7.

Listing 6.7: Passing by Value (MyClassArgument.java)

```
public class MyClassArgument
{
  public static void myMethod(int i)
  {
    i++;
  }

  public static void main(String args[])
  {
    int i = 10;
```

```
    myMethod(i);
    System.out.println("The value of i is " + i );
  }

}
```

What value would be printed out? The variable "i" was passed to my-Method and then increased by one. Would the program print out 10 or 11? That depends on if "i" was passed by reference or by value. Table 6.3 summarizes the differences between by reference and by value.

Learning Objective #6
Know the difference between "by value" and "by refernce".

By Value
By value arguments do not change the value of the calling variable.

By Reference
By reference arguments do change the value of the calling variable.

Table 6.3: The Difference Between by Reference and by Value

by reference	Any changes made to the argument inside of the method or function are reflected outside the method or function as well.
by value	A copy of the variable is made for the method, so any changes made to the argument inside of the method or function are not kept when the method or function returns.

Usually variables are passed by value in Java. When a non-object variable, such as an int, is passed to a method or function it is by value. So in the above example, myMethod would have no effect on the variable 1. The value 10 would be printed. Java does not allow you to choose when a variable is passed by reference or by value. It is governed by a set of rules. These rules are shown in Table 6.4.

Table 6.4: Is it by Value or by Reference

Type	By Value or by Reference
Primitive data types (i.e. ints)	by value
Object References	by value
Objects	by reference
Arrays	by reference

Some of these terms may not be familiar to you. Arrays will be covered in Chapter 6. Primitive data types are all of the built in non-object types supported by Java. Java supports eight primitive data types: byte, short, int, long, char, float, double and boolean.

It is important to understand the difference between an object and an object reference. An object is the actual memory image of the object. You can not directly access an object in Java, you must access it through object references. Objects in Java are always passed by reference, but their object references are always passed by value. To see the difference consider Listing 6.8.

Listing 6.8: By Value and By Reference (MethodCall.java)

```java
import javax.swing.*;

public class MethodCall
{

  static void changeValue(JButton button)
  {
// Change the text of the button, this
// new value is reflected outside of the
// call to "changeValue"
    button.setText("New value");
  }

  static void changeReference(JButton button)
  {
// Create a new button, and assign its
// reference to "button". This change is
// not reflected outside of the call
// to "changeValue"
    button = new JButton("New value");
  }

  static void changePrimitive(int i)
  {
    i = i + 1;
  }

  /**
   * Main entry point for example.
   * @param args Not used.
   */
  public static void main(String args[])
  {
    // setup the variables
```

```
    JButton button1 = new JButton("Old Value");
    JButton button2 = new JButton("Old Value");
    int var = 5;

    // call the methods
    changeValue(button1);
    changeReference(button2);
    changePrimitive(var);

    // display the new values
    System.out.println("Button1:" +
      button1.getText());
    System.out.println("Button2:" +
      button2.getText());
    System.out.println("Primitive variable:" + var);
  }
}
```

In this example two object references are created button1 and button2. These references both point to two separate JButton objects. We will see more about JButton in Chapter 10. For now we only care about a text string that it holds. To change this text string you have to call JButton's setText method. If you want to get the text string back, you have to call JButton's getText method. This will allow you to see the difference between a modification to an object reference and a modification to the object itself.

When the button parameter is passed to "changeReference" and "changeValue", the button is passed by reference. Buttons are always passed by reference, because they are objects. However, inside of each method, you have the opportunity to change the button. The method changeValue changes the actual object, as it calls the setText method to change the object. Changes made by changeValue will be reflected outside of changeValue. The method changeReference will only change the reference, and its changes will not be reflected outside of the changeReference method.

Chapter Review

This chapter showed you how to create your own Java methods. You were shown how to create both static and nonstatic methods. Additionally, the difference between static and non static variables was explored. Most of the functions and methods you create will be nonstatic.

Variables can be of different scopes. This chapter showed you three different scopes that variables can be local variables, instance variables, and static instance variables. Local variables can only be accessed from within the method or function they were created in. Instance variables can be accessed from anywhere inside of the class. Static instance variables can be accessed from anywhere in the class, but they do not have a unique value for each instance. When you create instance variables, they will be nonstatic.

New Terms

By Reference Variables can be passed to methods and functions "by reference". If this is the case, then changes made to the argument in the method will remain after the method terminates.

By Value Variables can be passed to methods and functions "by value". If this is the case, then changes made to the argument in the method will not remain after the method terminates.

Class A class is an object data type provided by Java or the program.

Function A reusable block of code that can be called from elsewhere in the program. A function returns a value.

Instance Function A function that is not declared static. To access an instance function the class must have been instantiated with the "new" operator.

Instance Method A method that is not declared static. To access an instance function the class must have been instantiated with the "new" operator.

Instance Variable A variable that is not declared static. To access an instance variable the class must have been instantiated with the "new" operator.

Local Variable A variable that is local to a method or function. Any value assigned to the variable only has meaning in the method, and will lose its value when the method returns.

Method A reusable block of code that can be called from elsewhere in the program. A method does not return a value.

Object An instance of a class.

static A Java keyword that can be applied to a variable, method, function or other Java construct.

Static Function A function that is declared static. A static function can be accessed either through an instance or directly through the class.

Static Method A method that is declared static. A static function can be accessed either through an instance or directly through the class.

Static Variable A variable that is declared static. A static variable can be accessed either through an instance or directly through the class, if it is declared at the class level. If the static variable is declared in a function or method, then it will hold its value, even after the method terminates.

Review Questions

1. Is there anything wrong with the following class?

```
public class MyClass
{
  public void test()
  {
    System.out.println("Test");
  }

  public static void main(String args[])
  {
    test();
  }
}
```

2. What will be the output of this program? Why?

```
public class MyClass
{
  public static void test(int i)
  {
    i = i + 1;
  }

  public static void main(String args[])
  {
    int i = 10;
    test(i);
    System.out.println("i is " + i );
  }
}
```

3. What is the effect of placing the keyword "static" in front of a local variable?

4. Do the terms class and object mean the same thing? If not, what is the difference.

5. Can the main method access instance variables directly?

Assignment #6

Write a program, named Assignment6, that contains two instance variables named total and itemCount. These two variables will keep track of a total and number of items.

You should provide two methods. The first method, named clear will clear the total and item count. The second method, named add, will accept numbers to be added to the total.

Finally, you will provide two functions. The first, named "getTotal" will return the total. The second, named "getAverage" will return the average.

You should test your program with the following numbers. You can test your program by calling "add" in the main method.

17

22

48

22

1

5

What is the average? What is the total?

CHAPTER 7: MID TERM

Chapter 7 contains an example Mid Term Exam. Some questions will have more than one correct answer. Chapter 8 contains the answers, and a review of the correct answer.

1. Which of the following is a valid main method?

A> public static void main(String args[])

B> static void main(String args[])

C> public static void main()

D> public static int main(String args[])

2. Which company created Java?

A> Microsoft

B> Oracle

C> IBM

D> Sun Microsystems

3. How do you usually read a number from the user?

A>   Use the readNumber method.

B>   Use the inputNumber method.

C>   Use readLine to read in a string, and then convert that string to a number.

4. What does the command "javac" do?

A>   It compiles a Java program.

B>   It runs a Java program.

C>   It allows you to edit a Java program.

5. Given the following method declaration, what does "void" mean?
public void test()

A>   The statement "void" means that this method does not return any thing.

B>   It means that this method will return a variable of type void.

C>   It means that this method should no longer be used.

6. Can a static method can access nonstatic instance variables?

A>   Yes

B>   No

7. Which of the following would you most likely store inside of a String?

A>   The name of your father.

B>   The year that a person was born.

C>   The price of butter.

**8. Which of the following variable types can hold decimal places? (i.e. 3.13).
Choose all correct answers**

A>   byte

B>   short

C>   int

D>   long

E>   float

F>   double

9. Java programs must be compiled before they are run.

A>   True

B>   False

10. What happens when an Exception occurs inside of a try block, and there is a catch block that handles this sort of exception?

A>   The program terminates (crashes)

B>   An error message is displayed and the program continues.

C>   The program executes the catch block.

11. Which of the following variable types can be used with a switch/case block?
There may be more than one correct answer.

A>   String

B>   int

C>   double

D>   byte

E>   short

12. Which of the following would you most likely store inside of an int?

A>   The name of your mother.

B>   The price of a pound of cheese.

C>   The number of rooms in your home.

13. What happens when you compile a computer program?

A>   The program is deleted.

B>   Your program begins running.

C>   The source code is converted to a form that the computer can easily understand, and execute.

14. What is a .class file?

A>   It is what the compiler produces.

B>   You edit this file and put your Java source code here.

C>   Java does not use .class files.

15. What is the proper way to compare two strings: str1 and str2?

A>   if(str1==str2)

B>   if(str1=str2)

C>   if(str1.equals(str2))

16. What does the Java import statement do?

A>   Displays a line of text.

B>   Not a valid Java statement.

C>   Allows your program to use other classes.

17. Are Java variable names case sensitive?

A>   Yes.

B>   No

18. What should be at the end of each case statement?

A>   break;

B>   end case

C>   end if

19. Which of the following makes use of Java's single-line comment?

A> # Comment line 1

#comment line 2

B> // Comment line 1

// Comment line 2

C> – Comment line 1

– Comment line 2

D> /* Comment line 1

Comment line 2 */

20. Which of the following are valid types of Java applications? Choose all that are correct.

A> Console Application.

B> Java Applet

C> Mini Java application.

21. What is true of packages and classes?

A> Neither packages nor classes exist in Java, those words are meaningless.

B> Classes are placed inside of packages for larger projects.

C> Packages are placed inside of classes for larger projects.

22. What happens when you pass a bad number (i.e. "33jj2") to the Integer.parseInt method?

A> A NumberFormatException is thrown.

B> The method would return 0.

C> The method would return -1.

D> The method would return null.

23. If the variable str contains a string and the variable d contains a double, how do you convert str into a double?

A> d = str;

B> d = val(str);

C> d = Double.parseDouble(str);

24. What is the name of the first method that is executed? This is where your program begins.

    A>   start

    B>   startup

    C>   main

25. What can usually replace an if/else ladder?

    A>   Nothing, they are required.

    B>   A switch/case block.

    C>   A stair/case block.

CHAPTER 8: MID TERM REVIEW

Chapter 8 is a review the correct answers for the midterm exam, that was presented in Chapter 7.

1. Which of the following is a valid main method?

A>   public static void main(String args[])

B>   static void main(String args[])

C>   public static void main()

D>   public static int main(String args[])

Correct answer: A
The syntax for a Java main method is very specific. It must be static, void and accept an array of string arguments.

2. Which company created Java?

A>   Microsoft

B>   Oracle

C>   IBM

D>   Sun Microsystems

Correct answer: D
Sun Microsystems is the company that created Java.

3. How do you usually read a number from the user?

A>   Use the readNumber method.

B>   Use the inputNumber method.

C>   Use readLine to read in a string, and then convert that string to a number.

Correct answer: C
Input from the user always comes in String form.   So read it as a string and convert to a number.

4. What does the command "javac" do?

A>   It compiles a Java program.

B>   It runs a Java program.

C>   It allows you to edit a Java program.

Correct answer: A
The command javac compiles a .java file into a .class file.

5. Given the following method declaration, what does "void" mean?
public void test()

A>   The statement "void" means that this method does not return anything.

B>   It means that this method will return a variable of type void.

C>   It means that this method should no longer be used.

Correct answer: A
The keyword void, in this case, means that there is no return value. It means that test is a method, not a function.

6. Can a static method can access nonstatic instance variables?

A>   Yes

B>   No

Correct answer: B
Static methods cannot access nonstatic (or instance) variables.

7. Which of the following would you most likely store inside of a String?

A>   The name of your father.

B>   The year that a person was born.

C>   The price of butter.

Correct answer: A
The year a person was born would likely be an int, and the price of butter would be a float or double. Strings store text.

8. Which of the following variable types can hold decimal places? (i.e. 3.13). Choose all correct answers

A> byte

B> short

C> int

D> long

E> float

F> double

Correct answers: E and F
The float and double datatypes can hold decimal places. The others, listed here, do not hold decimal places.

9. Java programs must be compiled before they are run.

A> True

B> False

Correct Answer: A
Java programs must be compiled before they are run. There is no way to run Java source code.

10. What happens when an Exception occurs inside of a try block, and there is a catch block that handles this sort of exception?

A>   The program terminates(crashes)

B>   An error message is displayed and the program continues.

C>   The program executes the catch block.

Correct answer: C
When an exception occurs in a try block, the program does not crash. The only error message that will be displayed is one that the program might have in the catch block, and it is NOT required that you put an error message in the catch block. So C is the only correct answer.

11. Which of the following variable types can be used with a switch/case block?
There may be more than one correct answer.

A>   String

B>   int

C>   double

D>   byte

E>   short

Correct answers: B,D and E
Only numeric non-floating point datatypes can be used with the switch/case statements. Strings are not allowed either.

12. Which of the following would you most likely store inside of an int?

A> The name of your mother.

B> The price of a pound of cheese.

C> The number of rooms in your home.

Correct answer: C
You don't have half, or fractional, rooms in your house. So you want a whole number, which an int is perfect for.

13. What happens when you compile a computer program?

A> The program is deleted.

B> Your program begins running.

C> The source code is converted to a form that the computer can easily understand, and execute.

Correct answer: C
Your program is not deleted. Additionally, you can't run the program until its compiled, so C is the only logical choice.

14. What is a .class file?

A> It is what the compiler produces.

B> You edit this file and put your Java source code here.

C> Java does not use .class files.

Correct answer: A
Java programs are stored in .class files. These files are created when you compile your application.

15. What is the proper way to compare two strings: str1 and str2?

A> if(str1==str2)

B> if(str1=str2)

C> if(str1.equals(str2))

Correct answer: C
You should never compare two strings with = or double equal (==). You should always use String.equals.

16. What does the Java import statement do?

A> Displays a line of text.

B> Not a valid Java statement.

C> Allows your program to use other classes.

Correct answer: C
Allows your program to use other classes provided by Java, third party libraries, or other parts of your program.

17. Are Java variable names case sensitive?

A> Yes.

B> No

Correct answer: A
Yes, Java variable names are case sensitive.

18. What should usually be at the end of each case statement?

A> break;

B> end case

C> end if

Correct answer: A
Each case should generally always have a break, unless you are grouping several of them together.

19. Which of the following makes use of Java's single-line comment?

A> # Comment line 1

    #comment line 2

B> // Comment line 1

    // Comment line 2

C> – Comment line 1

    – Comment line 2

D> /* Comment line 1

    Comment line 2 */

Correct answer: B
Single line comments in Java start with //

20. Which of the following are valid types of Java applications? Choose all that are correct.

    A>   Console Application.

    B>   Java Applet

    C>   Mini Java application.

Correct answers: A and B
There is no such thing as a Mini Java application.

21. What is true of packages and classes?

    A>   Neither packages nor classes exist in Java, those words are meaningless.

    B>   Classes are placed inside of packages for larger projects.

    C>   Packages are placed inside of classes for larger projects.

Correct answer: B
A large program can organize its classes into packages.

22. What happens when you pass a bad number (i.e. "33jj2") to the Integer. parseInt method?

A> A NumberFormatException is thrown.

B> The method would return 0.

C> The method would return -1.

D> The method would return null.

Correct answer: A
Java throws a NumberFormatException when an invalid number is parsed.

23. If the variable str contains a string and the variable d contains a double, how do you convert str into a double?

A> d = str;

B> d = val(str);

C> d = Double.parseDouble(str);

Correct answer: C
To convert a string to a double, use the Double.parseDouble function.

24. What is the name of the first method that is executed? This is where your program begins.

> A>   start
>
> B>   startup
>
> C>   main

Correct answer: C
The main method is where Java starts an application.

25. What can usually replace an if/else ladder?

> A>   Nothing, they are required.
>
> B>   A switch/case block.
>
> C>   A stair/case block.

Correct answer: B
Switch/case can usually replace if/else ladders.

CHAPTER 9: USING LOOPS

In Chapter 9 you will learn about:
- For Loop
- While Loop
- Do/While Loop
- What are loops for

Computers are great at repetitive operations. If you teach a computer how to write a paycheck for one single employee, it is not much more complex to modify your program to produce paychecks for 100 employees.

To make a computer perform a task over and over you must use a loop. There are many different kinds of loops in Java, but they all accomplish essentially the same thing. Loops allow programs to repeat the same operation many times.

Consider the following steps, summarized in Table 9.1.

Table 9.1: Steps for a Typical Loop Application

Step 1	Set the variable employeeNumber to 1
Step 2	Print the paycheck for employeeNumber
Step 3	Increase employeeNumber by 1
Step 4	If the employee number is less than or equal to 100 go to step 2

This is a very simple loop. It will print paychecks for 100 employees. As you can see step 1 begins by setting the variable to the first employee. Loops will often have a control variable, such as this, that count up as the loop executes. For this loop, the variable employeeNumber is counting up.

Step 2 prints the paycheck for each employee. Next, the employee number is increased by one. Step 4 checks to make sure that the employee number has not gone too high, and if not goes back to step 2 to repeat the loop.

As you can see, the loop will continue executing until we have reached employee number 100. Figure 9.1 shows this same loop, expressed as a flow chart.

Figure 9.1: The Loop as a Flowchart

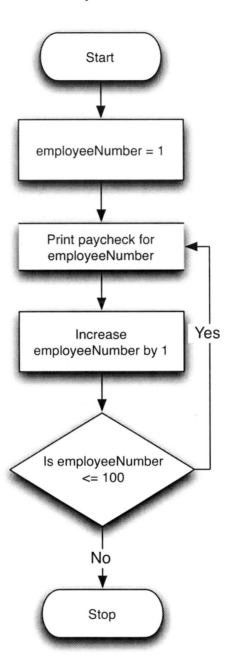

Java Loop Types

Java contains a total of three different loop types. Multiple loop types are not really needed, Java could have gotten by with only one loop type. However, having three different loop types allows you to choose a loop that works well for your intended use.

The three loop types Java contains are:

- While
- Do/While
- For

I will now show you how each of the loop types work.

The While Loop

First we will look at the "while" loop. The "while" loop will keep repeating a section of code until a condition is met. First, I will show you how to construct a "while" loop.

Constructing the While Loop

A While loop looks very similar to an "if statement". There is a condition, which must be "true" for the While loop to execute. Additionally, there is a block of code that will be executed so long as the "while" condition is true. Listing 9.1 shows what a typical "while loop" would look like.

Listing 9.1: A Typical While Loop (LoopExampleWhile.java)

```java
public class LoopExampleWhile
{
  public static void main(String args[])
  {
    int i = 1;

    while( i<=10 )
    {
      System.out.println("Loop:" + i );
      i = i + 1;
    }
  }
}
```

As you can see, the "while" loop contains an expression, in this case "i<=10". The "while" loop will repeatedly execute its body so long as i is less than 10.

When to use the While Loop

The while loop is probably the most commonly used of the Java loops. If you are ever unsure of what loop type to use, choose the while loop. As you will see in the next two sections, the other loop types are used for more specific purposes.

The Do/While Loop

The "do/while" loop is very similar to the "while" loop. The only difference is where the decision to continue looping is made. The "while" loop makes the decision at the beginning, whereas the "do/while" loop makes the decision at the end.

When would this make a difference? This will be examined in the next section.

When the Decision is Made

If the decision to is made at the top of the loop, such as the While loop, then your loop could end up executing zero times. It is possible to create a "while" loop that will execute zero times. Consider Listing 9.2.

Listing 9.2: A While Loop (LoopExampleWhile2.java)

```java
public class LoopExampleWhile2
{
  public static void main(String args[])
  {
    int i = 11;

    while( i<=10 )
    {
      System.out.println("Loop:" + i );
      i = i + 1;
    }
  }
}
```

How many times will the above source code execute? None! This is because the variable "i" starts out with a value of 11. The while loop will execute so long as the variable "i" is less than 10. Since the variable "i" started out greater than 10, the loop will never execute.

However, because a "do/while" loop makes the decision after the loop, your loop is guaranteed to execute a least once.

Consider Figure 9.2, which shows the flowchart of a While loop.

Figure 9.2: A While Loop as a Flowchart

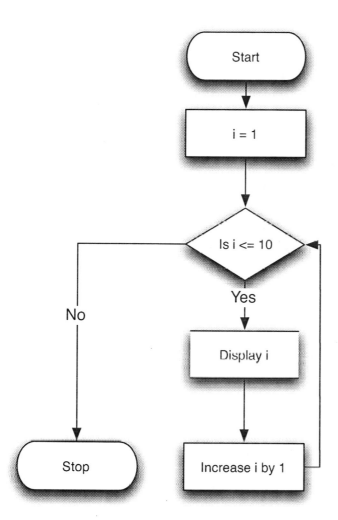

As you can see from the above figure, the decision to keep looping is made before any other action is taken. Figure 9.3 shows a "do/while" loop.

Figure 9.3: A "do/while" Loop as a Flowchart

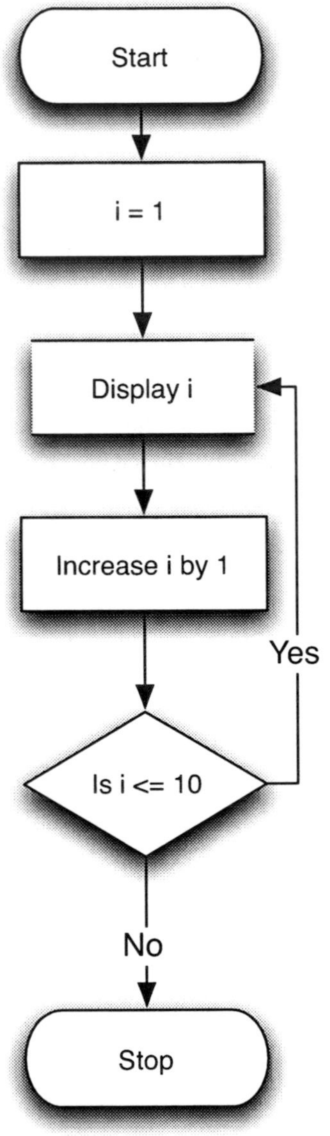

As you can see from the above figure, the decision to keep looping is made after the loop prints out its current number. Because of this, you can be sure that the loop will execute at least once.

Now I will show you how to construct a "do/while" loop.

Constructing the Do/While Loop

The "do/while" loop looks very similar to the while loop. Listing 9.3 shows a "do/while" loop.

Listing 9.3: A Do/While Loop (LoopExampleDoWhile.java)

```java
public class LoopExampleDoWhile
{
  public static void main(String args[])
  {
    int i = 1;

    do
    {
      System.out.println("Loop:" + i );
      i = i + 1;
    } while( i<=10 );
  }
}
```

When to use the Do/While Loop

The "do/while" loop is probably the least commonly used of the Java loops. The "do/while" loop should only be used when you want to make sure the loop executes once, or if you don't know the value ahead of time. Consider the following example, where you do not know the value ahead of time. Listing 9.4 shows a simple menu application.

Listing 9.4: A Simple Menu (LoopExampleMenu.java)

```java
import java.io.*;

public class LoopExampleMenu
{
  public static void main(String args[])
  {
    InputStreamReader inputStreamReader =
      new InputStreamReader ( System.in );
    BufferedReader stdin =
      new BufferedReader ( inputStreamReader );
    String response;

    try
    {
      do
```

```
        {
          System.out.println("A> Menu option a");
          System.out.println("B> Menu option b");
          System.out.println("C> Menu option c");
          System.out.println("Q> Quit");
          System.out.print("Select>");
          response = stdin.readLine();
        } while( !response.equals("q") &&
            !response.equals("Q") );
      }
    catch(IOException e)
      {
      }
    }
  }
}
```

Here you are presenting a list of menu items to the user. The "do/while" loop keeps displaying the menu until you quit. Here a do while makes sense, because you do not know what the user has typed yet while you are displaying the menu. Also, you will want to display the menu at least once. No decision on quitting the "do/while" loop is made until the very end on the while line. And here we say to quit if the user has entered either a lowercase or capital letter Q.

The For Loop

The "for" loop is perhaps the most complex of the Java loops. It is also commonly used, so it is important that you understand the "for" loop. A "for" loop is good when you know a specific range of numbers you want to count through, for example one through one hundred. I will now show you how to construct a "for" loop.

Constructing the For Loop

Listing 9.5 shows a "for" loop that will count from 1 to 10.

Listing 9.5: For Loop (LoopExampleFor.java)

```
public class LoopExampleFor
{
  public static void main(String args[])
  {
    for(int i=1;i<=10;i++)
    {
      System.out.println("Count:" + i );
    }
  }
}
```

The "for" loop has three distinct parts. First, the variable is set.

```
int i = 1;
```

This assigns the value of 1 to the variable "i". This is the starting value for the loop. Next the range of the loop is defined.

```
i<=10
```

This says that the loop will stop when the variable "i" is no longer less than or equal to ten. This means that the loop will count up to 10. Finally, the counter says what steps to count.

```
i++
```

This says that the variable "i" will be increased by one each time. If you wanted to count by two's you would use:

```
i+=2
```

You can also count backwards. Lets look at an example of a "for" loop that counts backwards. Listing 9.6 shows just such a loop.

Listing 9.6: Another For Loop (LoopExampleFor2.java)

```java
public class LoopExampleFor2
{
  public static void main(String args[])
  {
    for(int i=10;i>=1;i--)
    {
      System.out.println("Count:" + i );
    }
  }
}
```

Here you can see that the "for" loop would count backwards. The loop begins at ten and counts back, so long as the variable is greater than or equal to 1.

When to use the For Loop

"For" loops are used when you know the range you need to count through. For example, if you know you need to count from one to ten, a "for" loop is an ideal choice.

Nested Loops

Learning Objective #4
Placing one
loop inside of
another creates
a nested loop.

It is also possible to place one loop inside of another. For example, consider the following nested loop in Listing 9.7.

Listing 9.7: A Nested Loop (NestedLoop.java)

```java
public class NestedLoop
{
  public static void main(String args[] )
  {
    for( int outer = 1; outer<=10; outer ++ )
    {
      for( int inner = 1; inner<outer ; inner ++ )
      {
        System.out.print( " " + inner );
      }
      System.out.println("");
    }
  }
}
```

If this program were run, it would produce the following output.

```
1
1 2
1 2 3
1 2 3 4
1 2 3 4 5
1 2 3 4 5 6
1 2 3 4 5 6 7
1 2 3 4 5 6 7 8
1 2 3 4 5 6 7 8 9
```

To understand why this output is produced, first look at the "outer" loop. The outer loop will execute 10 times. This will cause there to be 10 rows. Next the inner loop is executed for each time the outer loop is executed. Each time through the inner loop will count up the outer loop. This is why you see just one number the first time, two the second, and so on.

Chapter Review

In this chapter you learned how to use loops. Loops are used to execute a block of code repeatedly. Java supports three kinds of loops. While loops are the most simple and will execute so long as a condition is true. "do/ while" loops are just like a while loop except that they decide late, and thus will execute at least once. "For" loops are good for when you want to count within a specific range. Finally, you learned about nested loops. Nested loops are loops that are contained within other loops.

New Terms

break   If a break is placed inside of a case statement, the execution for that case statement ends. If a break is placed inside of a loop, the loop terminates.

continue   The continue statement causes the current loop to jump back to the top of the loop, without processing the rest of the code in the loop's body.

Do/While Loop   The "do/while" loop is one of Java's three loop types. The "do/while" loop will execute its body one or more times so long as a condition is true. The main difference between the while and do/while loops is that the do/while is guaranteed to execute at least once.

For Loop   The for loop is one of Java's three loop types. The "for" loop will execute its body over a range of values, so long as a condition is true. The "for" loop may execute zero times, if its condition is not true.

Loop   A loop is a block of code that is executed until a condition is no longer true.

Nested Loop   A nested loop is a loop that is placed inside of another loop.

While Loop   The while loop is one of Java's three loop types. The while loop will execute its body one or more times so long as a condition is true. The main difference between the while and do/while loops is that the while is not guaranteed to execute at least once.

Review Questions

1. What will be the output from the following loop?

```
for( int i = 1; i<10; i++ )
{
  System.out.println( i );
}
```

2. What will be the output from the following loop?

```
int i = 2;
while( i<20 )
{
     System.out.println( i );
     i = i + 5;
}
```

3. What will be the output from the following loop?

```
int i = 100;
do
{
  System.out.println( i );
   i = i + 1;
} while( i<10 );
```

4. Write a loop (for, while or do/while) that will count from 2 to 10 by twos.

5. Rewrite the following "for" loop as a while loop.

```
for( int i = 1; i<=10; i++ )
{
  System.out.println( i );
}
```

Assignment #7

Write a program, named Assignment8, that will prompt the user for a height and width. The program should then display a rectangle, using the * character, that matches the specified dimensions.

For example, the program might be ran as follows:

```
Enter the width? 4
Enter the height? 3

****
****
****
```

Hint: A nested loop would be a great way to solve this assignment.

CHAPTER 10: STRINGS

In Chapter 10 you will learn about:
- **Strings**
- **Parsing Strings**
- **Searching Strings**
- **Substrings**

Strings are a very important concept in any programming language. Strings are variables that can hold textual data. We have already seen strings in previous chapters. However, in this chapter we will see how to process strings.

You may be wondering what exactly I mean by string processing. String processing means taking text, often entered by a user, and changing its appearance. A very simple example of this might be a website that prompts users for their first and last name. Many users, especially inexperienced typists, may enter their name in either all lower case, or perhaps all upper case. You could end up with several names improperly capitalized.

- jeff heaton
- John Smith
- JANE SMITH

You would not want to store a list of names like this. It does not look very professional to have the names entered like this. You can't just ask your users to enter their names with a consistent capitalization scheme, as users rarely do what they are told. The way to handle this is to have the computer modify each of the user names, stored as a string, into the correct capitalization rules.

In this chapter you will learn how to do that. You will learn to no longer think of a string as a block of characters/words but rather as individual characters that you can directly manipulate.

What are Strings Made Of

A string is made up of individual characters. That's actually where the name string comes from, a string of characters. Each character in a string has an index. This is a number that identifies this character's position. Think of it as a street address. Consider the string "Java is Fun". Listing 10.1 shows a program that counts the number of characters in this string.

Listing 10.1: Get the Length of a String (StringLength.java)

```java
public class StringLength
{
  public static void main(String args[])
  {
    String str = "Java is Fun";
    System.out.println( str.length() );
  }
}
```

Learning Objective #1
Get the length
of a string.

As you can see from the above program, a string is created that contains the text "Java is Fun". The program then calls a method called length. All strings have this method available. These methods will give you information about the string. The length method will return 11, which is the number of characters in the string "Java is Fun". Count the characters yourself, make sure you see 11. Make sure you count the spaces!

There are also methods that allow you to get to the individual characters of a string. Consider Listing 10.2.

Listing 10.2: Get a String as Characters (GetChars.java)

```java
public class GetChars
{
  public static void main(String args[])
  {
    String str = "Java is Fun";
    for( int i=0; i<str.length(); i++ )
      System.out.println("Character #" +
      i + " is " + str.charAt(i) );
  }
}
```

Very Important
An array index
always starts at
zero in Java.

Notice the example displayed here. Look at the For loop. The For loop is a little different than most loops that we have seen before. This For loop starts counting at 0, and it is counting forward (because of i++). However, look at when the loop stops. It will stop when the variable "i" is no longer less than the string's length. You don't have to count up to a fixed number, you can use a method, such as length, to tell the For loop how far to go.

Very Important! Notice how the loop starts at zero? String's always start at position zero.

The output from this program is as follows:

```
Character #0 is J
Character #1 is a
Character #2 is v
Character #3 is a
Character #4 is
Character #5 is i
Character #6 is s
Character #7 is
Character #8 is F
Character #9 is u
Character #10 is n
```

Here you can see how the string is made up, there are 11 indices, ranging from zero through ten. Index nine, for example, contains the letter "u".

This is the purpose of the charAt method. For any index that you give charAt, it will return the character at that index.

Very Important! Don't give charAt too large of a value. If you have a string of length 5 then only index values 0,1,2,3 and 4 are valid. If you request index 5 or higher, an exception will be thrown and your program will crash.

Taking Sections of Strings

In the last section we saw that a string is made up of individual characters. In this section we will see that you can access parts of these strings and make new strings.

Learning Objective #2
Obtain substrings of the string.

Consider again the string "Java is Fun". What if we wanted to create a new string that just contained the word "is"? If you look at the above output, you will see that the word "is" takes up index positions 5 through 6. Java provides a method to allow you to grab a string that ranges between two index positions. This method, named substring, is used in Listing 10.3.

Listing 10.3: Separate a String (SubString.java)

```
public class SubString
{
  public static void main(String args[])
  {
    String str = "Java is Fun";
    String newstr = str.substring(5,7);
    System.out.println( newstr );
  }
}
```

The above program uses substring to grab everything from index position 5 through index position 7. You may have expected index position 6 to have been the end, since the variable "is" only takes up character positions 5 and 6. However, substring does not include the ending character.

Very Important! The substring method does not return the ending character of its range. Calling substring(5,7) grabs every character from 5 up to, but not including, 7.

Also very important! If you request characters outside of the range of the string, an out of bounds exception will be thrown. For example if the string contains "Test" and you call substring(10,20) an error will occur because character position 10 is invalid in a four character long string like "Test".

Searching Strings

Often, you will need to search a string. For example, if you wanted to remove all of the spaces from a string, you would have to search for the spaces, and remove them. Java provides a method that will show you what index a character is at. For example, if you searched the string "Java is Fun" for the first space, the index 4 would be returned.

The following example searches for, and displays, the index of the first space in the string. This is shown in Listing 10.4.

Listing 10.4: Find the Space in a String (FindSpace1.java)

```
public class FindSpace1
{
  public static void main(String args[])
  {
    String str = "Java is Fun";
    int i = str.indexOf(" ");
    System.out.println( "The space is at: "+i );
  }
}
```

As you can see, the above program calls a method called indexOf. This method returns the index of the first space. If it doesn't find what it is looking for, indexOf will return a value of "-1".

When this program is executed it will display "4".

Sometimes you may want to find the second, third, or some other space in a string. To do this you can provide indexOf with a starting index. For example, the following code searches for the first space, after index 5. Listing 10.5 shows this.

Listing 10.5: Find More Space in a String (FindSpace2.java)

```java
public class FindSpace2
{
  public static void main(String args[])
  {
    String str = "Java is Fun";
    int i = str.indexOf(" ",5);
    System.out.println( "The space is at: "+i );
  }
}
```

The above code displays a "7". This is because the search for the space does not start until index position 5.

Now that you understand how to use some of the string methods, lets use them together to do more complex operations on strings.

Removing a Single Character

First we will write a method of our own to remove a single character from a string. This method will take a string and an index, and remove that index character from the string. This program is shown in Listing 10.6.

Listing 10.6: Remove a Single Character (RemoveChar.java)

```java
public class RemoveChar
{
  public static String removeChar(String str,int i)
  {
    String first = str.substring(0,i);
    String last = str.substring(i+1,str.length());
    str = first+last;
    return str;
  }

  public static void main(String args[])
  {
    String str = "Java is Fun";
    str = removeChar(str,5);
    System.out.println(str);
  }
}
```

When executed, the above program will output "Java s Fun". This is because the program removes the fifth character from the string. But how exactly does it do this?

The removeChar method first breaks the string into two smaller strings. The first string, named "first" will contain everything in the string before the character to be removed. In this case, it will contain "Java ". The second string, named "last" will contain everything after the character to be removed, in this case "s Fun". Finally the two strings are combined and returned. The resulting string is the same as the original, only with the specified character removed.

Removing all of the Spaces from a String

Now we will tie together everything from this chapter and see a string example that uses most of the methods covered in this chapter. This program will take a string and remove all of the spaces from that string. Listing 10.7 shows this program.

Listing 10.7: Remove all Space from a String (RemoveSpace.java)

```
public class RemoveSpace
{
  public static String removeChar(String str,int i)
  {
    String first = str.substring(0,i);
    String last = str.substring(i+1,str.length());
    str = first+last;
    return str;
  }

  public static String removeSpace(String str)
  {
    int i=0;
    while( i<str.length() )
    {
      if( str.charAt(i)== ' ' )
      {
        str = removeChar(str,i);
      }
      else
      {
        i++;
      }
    }
    return str;
  }

  public static void main(String args[])
  {
```

```
    String str = "Now is the time for all good men to
come to the aid of their country.";
    str = removeSpace(str);
    System.out.println(str);
  }
}
```

The above program is made up of two primary methods. The first, named "removeChar", was first introduced in the previous section. This method will remove a single character from the specified string.

The second method, named "removeSpace", is called to remove all spaces from a string. It does this by looping over every character in the string. The while loop begins at position 0 and continues to the length of the string.

Each character in the string is compared to see if it is a space. If a character is found to be a space, then it is passed to removeChar to be removed. Once the while loop has reached the last character in the string, there is nothing more to check. At this point the program returns the new string, with the spaces removed.

There are many additional programs you can create to modify strings. For example you may want to create a program that takes phone numbers, such as they are formatted in the United States of America, an reformat them to only numbers. For example (314) 555-1212 would be reformatted to 3145551212.

Chapter Review

In this chapter you saw how to process strings in Java. Java makes many methods available to you to process strings. The charAt method allows you to access individual characters. The indexOf method will search the string for occurrences of other strings or characters. The substring method will break the string up into smaller substrings.

A string is used to hold textual values. A string is really just a collection of characters. By using the charAt method you can easily access the characters that make up a string. Each character in a string has a numeric index. All strings start with index 0.

New Terms

charAt The charAt function is a part of the String class. It is used to obtain an individual character inside of a string, at a specific index.

Character A character is the building block of the string. Individual characters, which usually correspond to keys on the keyboard, make up strings.

indexOf The indexOf function is a part of the String class. It is used to search the string for substrings or characters.

length The length function is a part of the String class. It is used to obtain the length of a string.

Parse Parsing is the process where the computer processes a string and converts it into a form that the computer can understand. For example, parsing a telephone number would likely involve removing any hyphen and parenthesis characters form the string and leaving only digits.

substr The substr function is a part the String class. It is used to break the string into smaller "substrings".

String A String is a Java datatype that holds text information. A string is made up of individual characters.

Review Questions

1. What will be the output from the following code?

```
String str = "Hello World"
System.out.println( str.subString(2,2) );
```

2. What will be the output from the following code?

```
String str = "Java";
System.out.println( str.charAt(1) );
```

3. What will be the output from the following code?

```
String str = "Hello World";
System.out.println( str.indexOf(' ') );
```

4. What is the difference between a string and a character? What would you store in a string? A character?

5. What is the result of running the following code?

```
String str = "Java";
System.out.println( str.charAt(4) );
```

Assignment #8

Write a program that will prompt the user for a USA phone number in the form (xxx) xxx-xxxx. Parse this 10-digit phone number to just a 10 digit string.

For example, the program might be executed as follows:

```
What is your phone number? (314) 555-1212
That has been parsed to: 3145551212
```

CHAPTER 11: ARRAYS

In Chapter 11 you will learn about:
- **Using Arrays**
- **Creating Arrays**
- **Looping Over Arrays**

In this Chapter you will learn about arrays. First, let's look at exactly what an array is. An array is a single type, such as a string. However, rather than just one string value, an array can hold many values. Let me show you a simple example of when you might need an array. Consider a program that holds a list of all of the students in my class, as seen in Listing 11.1.

Listing 11.1: A List Without Arrays (StudentList1.java)

```java
public class StudentList1
{
  public static void main(String args[])
  {
    // first enter all students
    String student1 = "Smith, John";
    String student2 = "Jones, Bill";
    String student3 = "Thomson, Jerry";

    // second print out all students
    System.out.println( student1 );
    System.out.println( student2 );
    System.out.println( student3 );
  }
}
```

As you can see, this very simple program creates a new String variable for each student added. There are several problems with this. For one, you have to know how many students you are going to have when the program is created and compiled. For a program to be useful, it must adapt its number of variables as you add new students. This is what arrays are for. You can create a single variable, named studentList, and add new students into this list.

Introducing Arrays

Arrays allow you to create a single variable that contains a set number of entries. You can then access these variables with a numeric address. You can think of these addresses much like street addresses. Consider a small town that has a Main Street with 20 houses on it. There is one entity, named Main Street, but there are 20 addresses: 1 Main Street, 2 Main Street, 3 Main Street, and so on. This is exactly how an array works.

I will begin with how an array is created.

Learning Objective #1
How to create
an array.

Creating Arrays

Arrays have individual types, such as string, int, etc. If you declare an array to be of type "String", then this is an array of strings. If you declare an array to hold int's then this string will hold int's. You can't mix and match. If you create an array of type "String", you can't put an int into the array.

Note: When you become more advanced with Object Oriented Programming, there are ways that you can store more than one type of variable in an array. However, this is beyond the scope of this book.

There are three steps involved in creating an array.

- Declare the Array
- Instantiate the Array
- Initialize the Array

I will now show you how to perform each of these operations.

Learning Objective #2
Declare an array.

Declare an Array

The first step in creating an array is to declare that array. In this step you are assigning the array its type and name. Nothing else about the array is communicated in this step. Listing 11.2 shows a program that declares an array that will hold strings.

Listing 11.2: Declare an Array (StudentList2.java)

```
public class StudentList2
{
  public static void main(String args[])
  {
    String studentList[];
  }
}
```

As you can see, the above program declares an array of strings. This looks almost the same as when we declare a string, except for the [] on the end of the string name. This indicates that this is an array. Now, rather than one single string you may have many strings. How many? Well, at this point zero. Just declaring the array is not enough. You should not start using the array until after you have instantiated it. Instantiating an array is when you define the length of the array.

Very Important! You must instantiated an array before you use it. If use the array before it is instantiated, an exception will be thrown.

Instantiate an Array

I will now show you how to instantiate an array. Instantiating an array is where the array size is defined. The following program builds on the last program by adding a line to instantiate the array. This program is shown in Listing 11.3.

Learning Objective #3
Instantiate an array.

Listing 11.3: Instantiate an Array (StudentList3.java)

```
public class StudentList3
{
  public static void main(String args[])
  {
    String studentList[];
    studentList = new String[3];
  }
}
```

As you can see, one additional line was added to this program from the list. Here it looks as if we are assigning a value to the studentList variable. In a way, that is what we are doing. We are creating a new array and assigning it to the studentList variable. The array has now been created, and using the array will no longer throw an exception. The next step is to put some values into the array.

Initializing an Array

Once the array has been created, it does not yet hold any useful data. In the case of an array of strings, the array holds only empty strings. If the array were a numeric type, it would hold only zeros at this point. Now, we must put some initial values into the array. This step is called initialization. Listing 11.4 shows the student list program modified to initialize the array.

Learning Objective #4
Initialize an array.

Listing 11.4: Initialize an Array (StudentList4.java)

```
public class StudentList4
{
  public static void main(String args[])
```

```
    {
      String studentList[];
      studentList = new String[3];
      studentList[0] = "Smith, John";
      studentList[1] = "Jones, Bill";
      studentList[2] = "Thomson, Jerry";
    }
}
```

As you can see, the program has been modified to store some values in the array. Notice how the array is indexed. You use the value [1] to access array element 1. You can put any number you like in there to specify which number you want in the array. However, you must be careful to not use a value that is larger than the size of the array. If you use too large of a value, an exception will be thrown and your program will crash.

Very Important
Arrays always start at index zero.

You should also notice which array elements I used. I used index 0,1 and 2. This is an array of size 3. So the only valid elements are 0,1 and 2. Using element 3 would thrown an exception.

Very Important! Arrays always begin at index 0 and run to one before the size of an array. For example an array of size 5 would have valid elements from 0 through 4. Using array element 5 would throw an exception.

Now that I have shown you how to create an array, it is time to see how to make use of them.

Using Arrays

In the previous section you saw how to create an array. Arrays can become very powerful when you use them to access large amounts of data. By allowing you to specify an index you can do many things with arrays that you could not with regular variables. As you will see later in this section you can use a loop to process all elements of the array. This allows you to quickly implement a global array operation, like printing out the array, with only a few lines of code.

I will begin by showing you how to access individual array elements.

Accessing Array Elements

Array elements can be accessed in much the same way as they are initialized. Just as the following line initializes array index 0.

```
studentList[0] = "Smith, John";
```

So too, does the following line print out the value of array index 0.

```
System.out.println( studentList[0] );
```

As you can see you use array element just like any other string. The only difference is you must always specify which index you want to use.

Listing 11.5 shows the how to print out the three students.

Listing 11.5: Print out a List of Students (StudentList5.java)

```
public class StudentList5
{
  public static void main(String args[])
  {
    String studentList[];
    studentList = new String[3];
    studentList[0] = "Smith, John";
    studentList[1] = "Jones, Bill";
    studentList[2] = "Thomson, Jerry";

    // now print the students
    System.out.println( studentList[0] );
    System.out.println( studentList[1] );
    System.out.println( studentList[2] );
  }
}
```

As you can see this program prints out each of the students. However, this program prints them out each with a separate println. What if there were 100 students? If there were, we would need 100 println's. There is a much better way to do this, which only requires one println. I will show you how to do this in the next section.

Using Loops with Arrays

Learning Objective #5
Using loops
with arrays.

As you have seen in previous sections, you can access individual array elements using the []'s. So far we have only accessed elements with fixed numbers, such as studentList[2]. This is only the beginning. You can also access array elements with variables, for example studentList[i]. If i held the value 2, then this would access array element 2.

In the last section we modified the student list program to print out the students. However, this print section requires one println for each student. This would not be efficient if we had a large number of students. Also, what if we only had 2 students? The program would have to be modified to handle this new number of students. Listing 11.6 shows a version of this program that uses a "for loop" to print out the students.

Listing 11.6: List Students with Loop (StudentList6.java)

```
public class StudentList6
{
  public static void main(String args[])
  {
    String studentList[];
    studentList = new String[3];
    studentList[0] = "Smith, John";
    studentList[1] = "Jones, Bill";
    studentList[2] = "Thomson, Jerry";

    // now print the students
    for( int i=0;i<3;i++ )
    {
      System.out.println( studentList[i] );
    }
  }
}
```

As you can see the students are now printed out with a for loop. Now no matter how many students you have, you can print them all out with the four lines occupied by the for loop.

Array Example Program

Now we will begin developing a more complex version of the student list. This is a lengthy example that will be developed in stages over the next three chapters. This will be a student list program that allows students to be added, removed and listed from an array. The version of this program for this chapter is shown in Listing 11.7.

Listing 11.7: Array Example Program (StudentList7.java)

```
import java.io.*;

public class StudentList7
{
  // used to read from the user
  static BufferedReader in;

  // how many students are there currently
  static int studentCount;

  // the student list
  static String studentList[];
```

```java
public static void addStudent()
{
  System.out.println("");
  System.out.println("*** Add Student ***");
  if( studentCount >24 )
  {
    System.out.println(
      "There are already 25 students, "+
      "which is the most you can have.");
    return;
  }

  System.out.print("Enter student's first name> ");
  String first = readInput();
  System.out.print("Enter student's last  name> ");
  String last = readInput();

  String name = last + ", " + first;
  studentList[studentCount] = name;
  studentCount = studentCount + 1;

}

public static void deleteStudent()
{
  System.out.println("");
  System.out.println("*** Delete Student ***");
  if( studentCount == 0 )
  {
    System.out.println(
      "There are no students yet, "+
      "no one to delete.");
    return;
  }

  for(int i=0; i<studentCount; i++ )
  {
    System.out.println( (i+1) + ":" +
      studentList[i] );
  }

  System.out.print(
    "Which student number do you wish to delete> ");
  String str = readInput();
  int number = 0;
```

```
      try
      {
        number = Integer.parseInt( str );
      }
      catch( NumberFormatException e)
      {
        System.out.println(
          "You did not enter a valid number.");
        return;
      }

      if( number<1 )
      {
        System.out.println(
          "Student number must be at least 1.");
        return;
      }

      if( number>studentCount )
      {
        System.out.println(
          "Student number must be less than " +
          studentCount );
        return;
      }

      // now actually delete that student
      int i = number-1;
      while( i<studentCount )
      {
        studentList[i] = studentList[i+1];
        i = i + 1;
      }

      studentCount = studentCount - 1;

    }

    public static void listStudents()
    {
      System.out.println("");
      System.out.println("*** List Students ***");
      if( studentCount == 0 )
      {
        System.out.println(
          "There are no students yet.");
```

```
      return;
    }

    for(int i=0; i<studentCount; i++ )
    {
      System.out.println( studentList[i] );
    }
}

// a simple method that inputs a line from
// the user and returns it
public static String readInput()
{
  try
  {
    String input = in.readLine();
    input = input.trim();
    return input;
  }
  catch(IOException e)
  {
  }
  return "";// an error occured
}


public static void main(String args[])
{
  // setup the variables
  InputStreamReader inputStreamReader =
    new InputStreamReader ( System.in );
  in = new BufferedReader ( inputStreamReader );
  studentList = new String[25];
  studentCount = 0;

  // now display the main menu
  boolean done = false;

  while( done==false )
  {
    // print 25 blank lines to clear the screen
    for(int i=0;i<25;i++)
    {
      System.out.println("");
    }
```

```
System.out.println(
  "*** Student List Main Menu ***");
System.out.println("A> Add Student");
System.out.println("D> Delete Student");
System.out.println("L> List Students");
System.out.println("Q> Quit program");
System.out.print("Choose> ");

// prompt the user
String input = readInput();
input = input.toUpperCase();
char ch = input.charAt(0);
switch( ch )
{
  case 'A':
    addStudent();
    break;
  case 'D':
    deleteStudent();
    break;
  case 'L':
    listStudents();
    break;
  case 'Q':
    done = true;
    break;
  default:
    System.out.println(
      "Please choose a valid choice!");
}
System.out.println("");
System.out.print("[Press any Enter/Return]");
readInput();
    }
  }
}
```

This is the longest program that we have seen yet! But don't worry, it is built upon what we have already learned. If you remember all the topics from the previous sections, you probably already understand much of this program does. In the next few sections, I will review what each part of the program is for.

The readInput Method

This program makes use of several methods. One such method is the readInput method. This method will read a single line of input from the user and return that line as a string. The readInput method is shown in Listing 11.8.

Listing 11.8: Reading User Input

```
public static String readInput()
{
  try
  {
    String input = in.readLine();
    input = input.trim();
    return input;
  }
  catch(IOException e)
  {
  }
  return "";// an error occurred
}
```

As you can see from the above method, a string is returned. This method reads a line of text from the user, just as we have seen before, using the readLine method. However, by placing this code inside of a method, we do not have to reproduce the try/catch block every place that we want to read a line of text from the user. This is one of the main features of methods. They allow us to take several lines of commonly used code and isolate them inside of the method. These methods can then be reused.

This method also calls the trim method. This will remove any blank spaces that the user may enter at the end of the input. Finally, the string that the user has entered is returned. Using the method is very easy. Now anytime you want to read a line of text from the user you simply use the following line of code:

```
String str = readInput();
```

This also makes the program much shorter, and easier to read. Now you can insert this one line rather than setting up the entire try/catch block.

The Main Method

The main method does two things. First, it sets up the static instance variables, and secondly it performs the main loop. In this section we will examine how the static instance variables are setup, in the next section we will examine the main loop.

The main method begins with the following lines.

```
// setup the variables
InputStreamReader inputStreamReader =
  new InputStreamReader ( System.in );
in = new BufferedReader ( inputStreamReader );
studentList = new String[25];
studentCount = 0;
```

First, the input stream is setup. This is the same as in any program that has required user input, except that the "in" variable is now a static class-level variable, declared near the top of Listing 11.7. This allows it to be accessed anywhere in the program. If you need to review reading from the user, refer to Chapter 4. Next, the studentList variable is set to an array of size 25. Finally, the student count is set to zero. The studentCount variable will always contain the number of students

The Main Loop

The main loop of the program displays the main menu and prompts the user for which option they would like to perform. The main loop begins with the following lines of code.

```
// now display the main menu
boolean done = false;

while( done==false )
{
  // print 25 blank lines to clear the screen
  for(int i=0;i<25;i++)
  {
    System.out.println("");
  }
```

First, a while loop is started with the "done" variable. The while loop will continue so long as the "done" variable is false, which it was just set to. The program will loop, displaying the main menu, until done is false. This allows the program to keep running after the user has chosen one of the main menu options. Once the user finally chooses "Quit", the done variable will be set to true, and the program will terminate.

The main loop also displays 25 blank lines. This clears off anything that was on the screen previously, and makes the main menu more clear.

Next, the program displays the main menu to the user and prompts for a choice, as seen here.

```
System.out.println("*** Student List Main Menu ***");
System.out.println("A> Add Student");
System.out.println("D> Delete Student");
System.out.println("L> List Students");
System.out.println("Q> Quit program");
System.out.print("Choose> ");

// prompt the user
String input = readInput();
input = input.toUpperCase();
char ch = input.charAt(0);
switch( ch )
{
  case 'A':
    addStudent();
    break;
  case 'D':
    deleteStudent();
    break;
  case 'L':
    listStudents();
    break;
  case 'Q':
    done = true;
    break;
  default:
    System.out.println(
      "Please choose a valid choice!");
}
```

196 Java for the Beginning Programmer

First, the main menu is displayed. Then the user is prompted for a line of text. That line of text is converted to uppercase, otherwise we would have to compare against both 'A' and 'a' for add user. By converting the string to upper case we are only comparing against 'A'. Next we use a switch/case to decide which option the user wants to do. Each of the menu options has a method that carries it out. The switch/case decides which method needs to be called.

Adding a Student

Adding a student is somewhat simple. The addStudent method is shown here.

```
public static void addStudent()
{
  System.out.println("");
  System.out.println("*** Add Student ***");
  if( studentCount >24 )
  {
    System.out.println(
      "There are already 25 students, " +
      "which is the most you can have.");
    return;
  }

  System.out.print("Enter student's first name> ");
  String first = readInput();
  System.out.print("Enter student's last  name> ");
  String last = readInput();

  // put in "Lastname, First" format.
  String name = last + ", " + first;
  studentList[studentCount] = name;
  studentCount = studentCount + 1;

}
```

First the method checks to see if there are already 25 students. If there are, an error is displayed, and the method returns. Then the program prompts the user for the first and last name of the student. The first and last name are then combined into the form "Heaton, Jeff".

Next the student is added to the first available array element, and the student count is increased.

Deleting a Student

Deleting a student is somewhat more complex. This is done in several parts:

- Display a list of all students
- Prompt user for which student to delete
- Make sure the user entered a valid student
- Actually delete the student

To display a list of all students the following code is used

```
System.out.println("");
System.out.println("*** Delete Student ***");
if( studentCount == 0 )
{
  System.out.println(
    "There are no students yet, "+
    "no one to delete.");
  return;
}

for(int i=0; i<studentCount; i++ )
{
  System.out.println( (i+1) + ":" +
    studentList[i] );
}
```

First, a check is performed to see if there are any students. If there are no students, then there is nothing to display. If this is the case, the program will exit with an error message.

Next, the program loops through all students and displays each student, with a student number. The student number is the array index of that student plus one. We add one to the student number so that there is no student with the student number of zero. This is done mainly for looks. Most people are used to seeing lists that start with one, not zero.

Then, the method prompts the user for the student number to delete and validates that student number.

```
System.out.print("Which student number do you wish to
delete> ");
String str = readInput();
```

```
int number = 0;

try
{
  number = Integer.parseInt( str );
}
catch( NumberFormatException e)
{
  System.out.println(
    "You did not enter a valid number.");
  return;
}

if( number<1 )
{
  System.out.println(
    "Student number must be at least 1.");
  return;
}

if( number>studentCount )
{
  System.out.println(
    "Student number must be less than " +
    studentCount );
  return;
}
```

As you can see, the student number is first read in as a string. The string is then converted to an int. The NumberFormat exception is caught, just in case the user enters an invalid number. The number is checked to see if it is below 1 or above the total number of students. Either of these is an error and causes the method to return.

Finally, we actually delete the student. This is done with the following lines of code.

```
// now actually delete that student
int i = number-1;
while( i<studentCount )
{
  studentList[i] = studentList[i+1];
  i = i + 1;
}

studentCount = studentCount - 1;
```

Let me explain how this deletes a user, then I will show the same process more visually. The variable "i" is assigned to the array element that you want to delete. Remember, we added one to every array element to show the user, so we need to subtract one to balance that. If the user said to delete student 1, the first student, that is really array element 0, the first array element.

Then the program starts at the student to be deleted, and copies the next student to that position. This process is repeated for each student in the list. Consider the following students, in an array, as shown in Figure 11.1.

Figure 11.1: Remove a Name, Step 1

Array Index	Student Name
0	Heaton, Jeff
1	John, Smith
2	Jones, Larry
3	Miller, Beth

We are now going to delete the second student, who has array index 1. The first time through the while loop, the variable "i" will have the value 1. This will cause array element 2 (i+1) to be copied to array element 1 (i). This is shown in Figure 11.2.

Figure 11.2: Remove a Name, Step 2

Array Index	Student Name
0	Heaton, Jeff
1	John, Smith
2	Jones, Larry
3	Miller, Beth

This results in the array looking like Figure 11.3.

Figure 11.3: Remove a Name, Step 3

Array Index	Student Name
0	Heaton, Jeff
1	Jones, Larry
2	Jones, Larry
3	Miller, Beth

Now the variable "i" is incremented to 2. The same process is repeated, and element 3 (i+1) will be copied to element 2 (i). This is shown in Figure 11.4.

Figure 11.4: Remove a Name, Step 4

Array Index	Student Name
0	Heaton, Jeff
1	Jones, Larry
2	Jones, Larry
3	Miller, Beth

This results in the array looking like Figure 11.5.

Figure 11.5: Remove a Name, Step 5

Array Index	Student Name
0	Heaton, Jeff
1	Jones, Larry
2	Miller, Beth
3	Miller, Beth

The loop is now done, the studentCount variable is decreased by one, giving us the following list of students. This is seen in Figure 11.6.

Figure 11.6: Remove a Name, Step 6

Array Index	Student Name
0	Heaton, Jeff
1	Jones, Larry
2	Miller, Beth

Listing the Students

The last operation that we will examine is listing the students. This is probably the simplest of the operations. The listStudents method is shown here.

```
public static void listStudents()
{
  System.out.println("");
  System.out.println("*** List Students ***");
  if( studentCount == 0 )
  {
    System.out.println(
```

```
          "There are no students yet.");
       return;
   }

   for(int i=0; i<studentCount; i++ )
   {
     System.out.println( studentList[i] );
   }
 }
```

This method begins by checking to see if there are any students. If there are none, that is displayed and the method exits. If there are students then the method loops over the entire array and displays each student. The students are displayed in the order they were added. In the next chapter, we will learn to alphabetize them.

Chapter Review

In this chapter you learned about arrays. Arrays allow you to store many values under a single variable name. This allows you to loop over the variables and perform other operations on the array list.

Arrays are always of a given type. Arrays are accessed by numeric indexes. These indexes start at zero and end one short of the size of an array. For example, an array of size 5 would have indexes 0,1,2,3 and 4. If you were to try to access array element 5, an exception would be thrown.

In this chapter the "StudentList" example was demonstrated. This example program will be built upon in the next three class chapters. In this chapter you saw how to add, delete and list the students. This program used many previously learned techniques and showed how a complex program is built upon simple parts.

New Terms

array An array is a list of objects or primitive datatypes. Arrays start at index zero.

Declare A variable, or array, is declared when its name and type are given. For example "int i;" declares a variable of type "int", named "i".

index An index is a number that references a character position or array element. Both character positions and array elements start at index zero.

Instantiate An array or object is instantiated when the object is actually allocated using the "new" operator. An array or object must be declared before it can be instantiated.

Initialize An array or object is initialized when it is assigned a value. An array must be instantiated before it can be initialized.

Review Questions

1. What are the three steps necessary to use an array?

2. The following code would like to create an array of size 10 and set every array element to 5. Does it accomplish this?

```
public class MyClass
{
  public static void main(String args[])
  {
    int a[] = new int[10];
    for(int i = 0; <10; i++ )
      a[i] = 5;
  }
}
```


3. What does the following code try to do? Is it correct?

```
public class MyClass
{
  public static void main(String args[])
  {
    int a[] = new int[10];
```

```
    a[10] = 10;
  }
}
```

4. What must be done to remove one single element of an array?

5. What index do arrays start at?

Assignment #9

Write a program that will prompt the user for student scores between 0 and 100. Keep track of how many students have scored in each of the 10% bands. Display the number of students in each "band".

For example, the program might be ran as follows:

```
Enter a score(0-100, q to quit)? 200
Invalid score
Enter a score(0-100, q to quit)? 100
Enter a score(0-100, q to quit)? 95
Enter a score(0-100, q to quit)? 80
Enter a score(0-100, q to quit)? 82
Enter a score(0-100, q to quit)? 45
Enter a score(0-100, q to quit)? q


* * Score Summary * *

2 students scored between 90 and 100.
2 students scored between 80 and 89.
0 students scored between 70 and 79.
0 students scored between 60 and 69.
0 students scored between 50 and 59.
1 students scored between 40 and 49.
0 students scored between 30 and 39.
0 students scored between 20 and 29.
0 students scored between 10 and 19.
0 students scored between 0 and 9.
```

CHAPTER 12: USING ARRAYS

In Chapter 12 you will learn about:
- **Using Arrays**
- **Bubble Sorting**
- **Extending the Student List Example**

In this chapter we will build upon the last chapter by introducing a more complex example of using an array. You will be shown how to sort an array.

Sorting Arrays

Arrays store lists of items. However, often a list must be in a specific order. Consider the student list example in the last chapter. As you added more and more students to it the list gets harder to read because it is in no specific order. Whichever student was entered first, comes first. This would become very cumbersome if we had a large number of students in this list.

Learning Objective #1
Understand the bubble sort.

Introducing the Bubble Sort

There are many different ways to sort arrays. One of the most basic is the bubble sort. The bubble sort works by going over the list and looking at two items at a time. If these two items need to be swapped, then they are swapped. This continues until the bubble sort makes it through without performing any swaps. Lets look at an example of how this works. Consider the following names in unsorted order.

```
0:John
1:George
2:Simon
3:Alice
4:Betty
```

As you can see these names are not in alphabetical order. To implement the bubble sort, we look at the first two names at location 0 and 1. Are they in the right order? No they are not. So we swap them, and are left with:

```
0:George
1:John
2:Simon
3:Alice
4:Betty
```

Now we continue, we look at locations 1 and 2. Are they in the right order? Yes they are. What about 2 and 3? No they are not. So we swap them, and are left with:

```
0:George
1:John
2:Alice
3:Simon
4:Betty
```

Continuing onward. Are locations 3 and 4 in the right order? No they are not. So we swap them, and are left with:

```
0:George
1:John
2:Alice
3:Betty
4:Simon
```

We have reached the end, now we start all over. Are locations 0 and 1 in order. They are, but how about 1 and 2. No they are not. So we swap them, and are left with:

```
0:George
1:Alice
2:John
3:Betty
4:Simon
```

Continuing on, how about 2 and 3? No, not in order.   So we swap them, and are left with:


```
0:George
1:Alice
2:Betty
3:John
4:Simon
```

Continuing on, how about 3 and 4? They are in order. We are at the end again. Start from the top. Are 0 and 1 in order? No they are not.   So we swap them, and are left with:


```
0:Alice
1:George
2:Betty
3:John
4:Simon
```

Continuing on, how about 1 and 2? Not in order.   So we swap them, and are left with:


```
0:Alice
1:Betty
2:George
3:John
4:Simon
```

Now how about 2 and 3. They are in order. How about 3 and 4? They are in order too. Time to start from the top again.

Locations 0 and 1 are in order, so are 1 and 2, so are 2 and 3, and guess what! So is 3 and 4. We made it through one pass with no swaps, that means we're done, the array has been sorted.

Now that we have seen how the bubble sort works, we need to implement it as a program.

Alphabetizing Strings

Before we can begin sorting strings we must see how we can check and see if two strings are in order. This is not hard, as the String class provides a method to allow us to do this. This method works similar to the equals method, but in addition to telling us if the two strings are equal, this method will also tell us what order the two strings are in. This method is called "compareTo". The "compareTo" method is called like this.

```
if( strA.compareTo(strB)==0 )
{
  System.out.println("These two strings are equal.");
}
```

If the compareTo method returns a zero, the two strings are equal. There are three values the compareTo method can return:

- 0 if the two strings are equal
- a number less than 0, if strA comes before strB
- a number greater than 0, if strB comes before strA

Therefore, using the method "compareTo" we can easily determine if two strings are in order. If the two strings are in order, compareTo will return a value less than zero.

There is another issue we need to deal with. That is, how can we swap two strings. Given the following array:

```
str[0]  =  "First";
str[1]  =  "Third";
str[2]  =  "Second";
str[3]  =  "Fourth";
str[4]  =  "Fifth";
```

What command would swap elements 1 and 2? You can't just use the following:

```
str[1]  =  str[2];
str[2]  =  str[1];
```

This may seem logical, but as soon as you execute str[1] = str[2], the array would look like this:

```
str[0] = "First";
str[1] = "Second";
str[2] = "Second";
str[3] = "Fourth";
str[4] = "Fifth";
```

This is no good. What happened to "Third"? You just copied over it, its gone now and its not coming back. So you see you can't just copy when you want to swap two strings. So how do we swap two strings? Consider this real-world example. Look at figure 12.1, we have a glass of milk and a glass of orange juice.

Figure 12.1: A Glass of Milk and a Glass of Orange Juice

We want to swap them. We want the milk in the OJ's glass and vise versa. How can we do it? We can't just pour one glass into the other and expect it to work, much like we just tried with the array. Figure 12.2 shows how well that works!

Figure 12.2: This Does Not Work!

So how can it be done? What are we missing? Figure 12.3 shows.

Figure 12.3: A Spare Glass is Needed

We need a third glass. Using this third glass allows us to pour the milk into the third glass, then pour the OJ into the old milk glass, and finally pour the extra glass into the old OJ glass. Figure 12.4 shows this.

Figure 12.4: The Swap is Made

The program is no different. What we need is a temporary variable to hold the value during the swap, like so:

```
int temp - str[1];
str[1] = str[2];
str[2] = temp;
```

As you can see, str[1] is first copied into a temp variable. Next str[2] is copied into str[1]. Finally the temp variable is copied to str[2]. This completes the swap.

Implementing the Bubble Sort

Now I will show you how to implement a bubble sort. First we will examine the flowchart of a bubble sort. This flowchart is shown in Figure 12.5.

Figure 12.5: A Bubblesort Flowchart

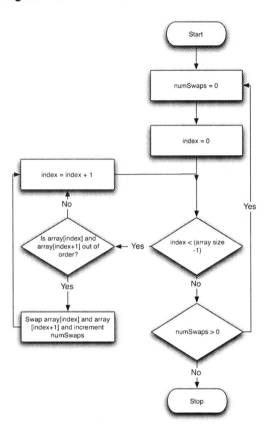

As you can see, the array is processed, swapping unordered pairs, until the program makes it through without making any swaps. Once the program makes no swaps the list is sorted.

Now I will show you how to implement this in Java code. Listing 12.1 shows the bubble sort.

Listing 12.1: The Bubble Sort (BubbleSort.java)

```java
class BubbleSort
{
  public static void bubbleSort(String data[],int
size)
  {
    boolean done = false;
    int index;
```

```
    while (done == false)
    {
      done = true;
      for (index=1 ; index < size;index++)
      {
        if (data[index].compareTo(data[index-1])<0)
        {
          // swap data[index] and data[index-1]
          String temp          = data[index];
          data[index]   = data[index-1];
          data[index-1] = temp;
          done = false;
        }
      }
    }
  }

  public static void main(String args[])
  {
    String str[] = new String[5];

    // unsorted array
    str[0]="John";
    str[1]="George";
    str[2]="Simon";
    str[3]="Alice";
    str[4]="Betty";

    // now bubble sort
    bubbleSort(str,5);

    // display the results
    for(int i=0;i<5;i++)
      System.out.println(str[i]);
  }
}
```

The program begins by filling the array with unsorted values. Then the bubbleSort method is called and the array is displayed. The resulting names are in alphabetical order.

If you examine the bubbleSort method you can see how it works. First a "done" variable is established. The "done" variable will remain false so long as at least one swap was made. To do this the "done" variable is first set to true, and then is set to false when the first swap occurs. If no swap occurs, the done variable remains true, and the loop exists.

Inside of the "while loop" a "for loop" is used to process every pair in the array. Each pair is checked, and if they are out of order, a swap occurs.

Adding Sorting to the Student List Example

Now we will add the bubble sort to the student example program. There really is very little modification to do. Listing 12.2 shows the completed application.

Listing 12.2: The Student List, with Bubble Sort (StudentList.java)

```java
import java.io.*;

public class StudentList
{
  // used to read from the user
  static BufferedReader in;

  // how many students are there currently
  static int studentCount;

  // the student list
  static String studentList[];

  public static void bubbleSort(String data[],
    int size)
  {
    boolean done = false;
    int index;

    while (done == false)
    {
      done = true;
      for (index=1 ; index < size;index++)
      {
        if (data[index].compareTo(data[index-1])<0)
        {
          // swap data[index] and data[index-1]
          String temp        = data[index];
          data[index]   = data[index-1];
          data[index-1] = temp;
          done = false;
        }
      }
    }
  }
}
```

```java
public static void addStudent()
{
  System.out.println("");
  System.out.println("*** Add Student ***");
  if( studentCount >24 )
  {
    System.out.println(
      "There are already 25 students, " +
      "which is the most you can have.");
    return;
  }

  System.out.print("Enter student's first name> ");
  String first = readInput();
  System.out.print("Enter student's last  name> ");
  String last = readInput();

  String name = last + ", " + first;
  studentList[studentCount] = name;
  studentCount = studentCount + 1;

  bubbleSort(studentList,studentCount);

}

public static void deleteStudent()
{
  System.out.println("");
  System.out.println("*** Delete Student ***");
  if( studentCount == 0 )
  {
    System.out.println(
      "There are no students yet, "+
      "no one to delete.");
    return;
  }

  for(int i=0; i<studentCount; i++ )
  {
    System.out.println( (i+1) + ":" +
      studentList[i] );
  }

  System.out.print(
    "Which student number do you wish to delete> ");
  String str = readInput();
```

```java
      int number = 0;

      try
      {
        number = Integer.parseInt( str );
      }
      catch( NumberFormatException e)
      {
        System.out.println(
          "You did not enter a valid number.");
        return;
      }

      if( number<1 )
      {
        System.out.println(
          "Student number must be at least 1.");
        return;
      }

      if( number>studentCount )
      {
        System.out.println(
          "Student number must be less than " +
          studentCount );
      }

      // now actually delete that student
      int i = number-1;
      while( i<studentCount )
      {
        studentList[i] = studentList[i+1];
        i = i + 1;
      }

      studentCount = studentCount - 1;

    }

  public static void listStudents()
  {
    System.out.println("");
    System.out.println("*** List Students ***");
    if( studentCount == 0 )
    {
      System.out.println(
```

```
        "There are no students yet.");
      return;
    }

    for(int i=0; i<studentCount; i++ )
    {
      System.out.println( studentList[i] );
    }
}

// a simple method that inputs a line from
// the user and returns it
public static String readInput()
{
  try
  {
    String input = in.readLine();
    input = input.trim();
    return input;
  }
  catch(IOException e)
  {
  }
  return "";// an error occured
}


public static void main(String args[])
{
  // setup the variables
  InputStreamReader inputStreamReader =
    new InputStreamReader ( System.in );
  in = new BufferedReader ( inputStreamReader );
  studentList = new String[25];
  studentCount = 0;

  // now display the main menu
  boolean done = false;

  while( done==false )
  {
    // print 25 blank lines to clear the screen
    for(int i=0;i<25;i++)
    {
      System.out.println("");
    }
```

```
System.out.println(
  "*** Student List Main Menu ***");
System.out.println("A> Add Student");
System.out.println("D> Delete Student");
System.out.println("L> List Students");
System.out.println("Q> Quit program");
System.out.print("Choose> ");

// prompt the user
String input = readInput();
input = input.toUpperCase();
char ch = input.charAt(0);
switch( ch )
{
  case 'A':
    addStudent();
    break;
  case 'D':
    deleteStudent();
    break;
  case 'L':
    listStudents();
    break;
  case 'Q':
    done = true;
    break;
  default:
    System.out.println(
      "Please choose a valid choice!");
}
System.out.println("");
System.out.print("[Press any Enter/Return]");
readInput();
    }
  }
}
```

As you can see, I added the bubbleSort method near the top. This is exactly the same bubbleSort method that was shown in the last listing. The only other change needed, is for the list to be resorted whenever a name is added. This is accomplished by adding a call to bubbleSort at the end of the addUser method.

Chapter Review

In this chapter you were shown an application of arrays. You saw how the bubble sort works and how to use it. The bubble sort works by looping over all element pairs in an array and swapping any elements that are out of order. This repeats until the bubble sort makes it through without swapping, once this happens the sort is done.

You saw how to compare two values. The compareTo method is used to do this. Given strA.compareTo(strB), compareTo returns 0 if the two strings are equal, a number less than 0, if strA comes before strB, or a number greater than 0, if strB comes before strA.

You were shown how to swap two variables. You can't just assign one variable to the other. You must use a temporary variable to hold one value during the swap.

New Terms

Bubble Sort A bubble sort is a method by which a list of items can be sorted. The bubble sort swaps pairs of items until the list is sorted.

compareTo The compareTo function is a part of the String class. It determines the placement of two strings. For example strA.compareTo(strB) would return 0 if the two strings are equal, a number less than 0, if strA comes before strB. Or a number greater than 0, if strB comes before strA

Swap A swap occurs when the contents of two variables must be exchanged. To properly swap two variables, a third, temporary variable is needed.

Temporary Variable A temporary variable is a variable that is used as a place holder for something for a very short time. A temporary variable is almost always a local variable.

Review Questions

1. How do you swap the values of two variables?

2. Describe how the bubble sort works.

3. Write out the bubble sort steps to sort the following list of numbers.

```
4  2  3  5  1
```

4. What would the following code display?

```
String strA = "A";
String strB = "B";

System.out.println( strA.compareTo(strB) );
```

5. What role does the temporary variable play in a bubble sort?

Assignment #10

Write a program, named Assignment11, that will prompt the user to enter a number of names. Then display the sorted result.

For example, the program might be ran as follows:

```
Enter a name (q to quit)? John
Enter a name (q to quit)? Paul
Enter a name (q to quit)? Jim
Enter a name (q to quit)? q

Sorted results:

Jim
John
Paul
```

CHAPTER 13: OBJECT ORIENTED PROGRAMMING

In Chapter 13 you will learn about:
- Object Oriented Programming
- Access Levels
- Getters and Setters
- Interfaces
- Insurance Example

In this chapter you will learn the basics of Object Oriented Programming.

Objects of Your Own

We have used objects in many of our programs so far. Anytime you use a String, you are using an object. However, we have yet to use any objects that we have created ourselves. In this chapter we will see how to create objects of our own.

Access Modifiers

You have already seen access modifiers. The most commonly used access modifier is public, which means that the variable or method can be accessed from anywhere. There are actually four access modifiers, of which public is one.

- public
- private
- protected
- (default)

Learning Objective #1
Understand the Java access modifiers.

Each of these access modifiers behave differently. It is important to note the last access modifier, you don't actually type the word "default" into the Java application. That just means that no access modifier was provided at all. For example, the following int declaration uses the default access modifier:

```
int i;
```

Do not assume that just because you did not specify an access modifier that it defaults to public or some other. No access modifier, is actually its own access modifier–which is called the "default" access modifier. If you had wanted to declare the above int as public, you should have used the following statement.

```
public int i;
```

The meaning of each access modifier is given in Table 13.1.

Table 13.1: Java Access Modifiers

Important
You never put the word default in for the default access. To declare "i" with default access just use:
int i;

Access Modifier	Description
public	Any other object's methods can access this variable or method.
private	Only methods in this class can access this variable or method.
protected	Only methods in this class, subclasses of this object can access the variable or method.
(default)	Other method's objects can access this method or variable if they are in the same package.

You may have noticed that I referred to a subclass of a class. This will be explained later in this chapter.

Creating the Base Class

To begin with, we will create a base class called "Person". This class is designed to be able to hold a person. It will contain only very basic information about this person.

- The person's first name
- The person's last name

Listing 13.1 shows a really simple form of this class.

Listing 13.1: A Simple Person Holder Class (Person1.java)

```
public class Person1
{
  public String first; // the person's first name
  public String last; // the person's last name
}
```

You will notice that this class has no main method. As a result this class can not be run, it will have to be used by another class that has a main method. This is the usual structure of a Java program. There will be many classes that make up the application, but only one will have a main method. A program, regardless of how many classes it has, will generally have only one main method. After all, you can only start from one place!

I will show you a main method that will take advantage of Person1 in a moment, but first, lets look at Person1. Person1, unfortunately, violates one of the key rules of object oriented programming. It has public instance level variables.

In object oriented programming you should never expose something as internal to a class as an instance variable. You should setup "gate keepers". These "gate keepers" will get the value of first and last for you. They will also set the value of first and last for you. The following shows how the Person class should actually be implemented.

Getters and Setters

The proper way to access instance variables is to use getters and setters. To do this, first, make all of your instance variables private, which means that only the class can access them. Then create a public method called getVariableName and setVariableName. The getVariableName method, called the getter, will return the value of the variable. The setVariableName method, called the setter, will set the value of variableName. Listing 13.2 shows the Person class with getters and setters.

Learning Objective #2
Understand getters and setters.

Listing 13.2: Using Getters and Setters (Person.java)

```
public class Person
{
  private String first; // the person's first name
  private String last; // the person's last name

  public void setFirst(String theFirst)
  {
    first = theFirst;
  }
```

```
        public String getFirst()
        {
          return first;
        }

        public void setLast(String theLast)
        {
          last = theLast;
        }

        public String getLast()
        {
          return last;
        }
}
```

As you can see both the "first" and "last" variables are declared as private. This means that they can only be accessed from within the Person class. But this is okay because we provide getters and setters to allow other classes to both get the value of first and last, as well as set the value of first and last.

The two getters, named "getFirst" and "getLast" both return the value of first and last. The two setters, named "setFirst" and "setLast" both set the value of first and last.

Using Objects

Next I will show you how to make use of your newly created object. The following class, shown in Listing 13.3 shows how to use the Person class.

Listing 13.3: Test the Person Class (TestPerson.java)

```
public class TestPerson
{
  public static void main(String args[])
  {
    Person personA = new Person();
    Person personB = new Person();

    personA.setFirst("John");
    personA.setLast("Smith");

    personB.setFirst("Jimmy");
    personB.setLast("Jones");

    // now display the two
```

```
System.out.println( personA.getLast() + ", " +
  personA.getFirst() );
System.out.println( personB.getLast() + ", " +
  personB.getFirst() );
  }
}
```

As you can see, the above class creates two Person objects. Notice how the getters and setters are used. Each object, personA and personB, have their own first and last names. First the setters are used to give the objects their values. Then the getters are used when the objects are to be displayed.

Subclassing Classes

In the previous example you saw how to create a basic object, with getters and setters. While this is the basic construct of object oriented programming, there is much more to object oriented programming than that. Next, I will show you how to subclass an object.

Creating an Exception Class

First we will create an exception class. We have seen that exceptions are thrown when things go wrong. This time, we're going to create an exception of our own. This exception is called TypeException. It will occur when the Student class, which will be created in the next section, is given an invalid type. The valid types for student are: Freshman, Sophomore, Junior, Senior and Graduate. If the type is set to anything other than one of these types, the TypeException will be thrown. Listing 13.4 shows the TypeException.

Listing 13.4: The TypeException (TypeException.java)

```
public class TypeException extends Exception
{
  TypeException(String message)
  {
    super(message);
  }
}
```

The TypeException is a subclass of the "Exception" class. You can see this by examining the class line. Notice the "extends Exception"? This indicates that the TypeException class is a subclass of the "Exception" class. This class will be used in the next section.

Java for the Beginning Programmer

When you subclass from another class you inherit all of the methods and properties of that class. By inheriting from the "Exception" class the new "TypeException" class can function as an exception.

Creating the Student Class

Now that the person and exception classes have been created, it is time to create the student class. The student class is a child, or subclass, of the person class. That is the Student will be the child of Person, and Person will be the parent class of Student. You can create other children of Person, for example you might want to create an Instructor class that also subclasses Person. Listing 13.5 shows the Student class.

Listing 13.5: The Student Class (Student.java)

```
public class Student extends Person
{
  private int studentNumber;
  private String type;

  public void setStudentNumber(int theStudentNumber)
  {
    studentNumber = theStudentNumber;
  }

  public int getStudentNumber()
  {
    return studentNumber;
  }

  public void setType(String theType)
  throws TypeException
  {
    if( !theType.equalsIgnoreCase("Freshman") &&
        !theType.equalsIgnoreCase("Sophomore") &&
        !theType.equalsIgnoreCase("Junior") &&
        !theType.equalsIgnoreCase("Graduate") &&
        !theType.equalsIgnoreCase("Senior") )
      throw new TypeException(
        "Invalid type: must be Freshman, Sophomore, "
        +"Junior, Senior or Graduate");
    type = theType;
  }

  public String getType()
  {
```

```
      return type;
   }
}
```

The subclass Student inherits everything from Person. As a result of this, the Student class contains a "first" and "last" name attributes. It also includes the two new attributes from the Student class: studentNumber and type. The "type" attribute specifies what type of student this is, namely: Freshman, Sophomore, Junior, Senior or Graduate.

The setter for the "type" attribute also validates that you are setting it to one of the accepted types. If you are not, the TypeException is thrown. Also notice the "throws" statement just below the setType method header. Any exceptions that you throw in a method must be listed on the "throws" statement.

Using Subclasses

Now that we have created the "Student" class, we should write a short class to test it. This class, named "TestStudent," is shown in Listing 13.6.

Listing 13.6: Test the Student Class (TestStudent.java)

Learning Objective #4
Understand how to create subclasses.

```
public class TestStudent
{
   public static void main(String args[])
   {
     Student student = new Student();
     try
     {
       student.setFirst("John");
       student.setLast("Smith");
       student.setStudentNumber(1);
       student.setType("Freshman");

       // now print it
       System.out.println(
           "Student: first=" + student.getFirst() +
           "last=" + student.getLast() +
           "studentNumber=" +
           student.getStudentNumber() +
           "type=" + student.getType() );

       // now cause an exception
       student.setType("Unknown");
     }
     catch(TypeException e)
     {
       System.out.println("Error:" + e.getMessage() );
     }
   }
}
```

This program creates a new student, named "John Smith". First, the student is created with a valid type. Then the student is displayed. Finally, the program sets the type to an invalid value and causes the TypeException to be thrown. The "Student" class will be used in the next chapter.

Understanding Interfaces

In addition to classes Java also contains interfaces. In this section you will be introduced to the concept of interfaces, as well as what they are used for.

What is an Interface

An interface is a class template. It defines all of the methods that are made available by that class. Why would you want to use an interface? Let me give you a real-world example.

You read about a new car in the news paper. It sounds like everything you've been looking for, so you rush out to your local car dealer and take a test drive. But wait. Sure you've been driving your last car for 5 years, but do you know how to drive this new one? After all, you've never sat behind the wheel of this car before, how do you know you can drive it? You know you can drive it because all cars follow a standard, in how they are operated. You know that you will turn the key, shift into reverse or drive, hit the pedal and go. It doesn't matter if its an electric car, hybrid car, or even a jet car. If it supports the "standard car interface", you can drive it!

This is what an interface is. You create a interface that specifies methods and tells how to operate a class. Then ANY class that supports this interface must be operated in the same way. Even if your program has never seen a class that supports a known interface, your program can support that class.

Implementing an Interface

To demonstrate interfaces I will show you a simple insurance application. I will create an interface named Payable. This interface means that the class knows how to pay a claim. The Payable interface is shown in Listing 13.7.

Listing 13.7: The Payable interface (Payable.java)

```
interface Payable
{
  public double getBenefit();
}
```

As you can see, the Payable interface defines one method. This method, named "getBenefit," will get the "death benefit" for this life insurance policy. There are many different life insurance policies, and they all calculate the "death benefit" a little different, this will not matter. You know that if the Policy class supports the Payable interface, you can support it.

Using Interfaces

I will now show you how to construct a simple application that supports the Payable interface. We will begin by creating a "Policy" base class. This class will be the parent class for many different types of life insurance policies. This class is shown in Listing 13.8.

Listing 13.8: The Policy Base Class (Policy.java)

```java
public class Policy
{
  private double face;
  private double premium;
  private String insured;
  private String beneficiary;

  public double getFace()
  {
        return face;
  }

  public void setFace(double d)
  {
        face = d;
  }

  public double getPremium()
  {
        return premium;
  }

  public void setPremium(double d)
  {
        premium = d;
  }


  public String getInsured()
  {
        return insured;
  }
```

```
public void setInsured(String s)
{
        insured = s;
}

public String getBeneficiary()
{
        return beneficiary;
}

public void setBeneficiary(String s)
{
        beneficiary = s;
}
}
```

The policy class is pretty simple. It supports several attributes, which all life insurance policies share. The attributes are shown in Table 13.2.

Table 13.2: Attributes of the Policy Class

Property	Description
face	The face value of the insurance policy (i.e. $100,000).
premium	The amount of money that the owner pays per month for the policy (i.e. $35).
insured	The person who's life is insured.
beneficiary	The person who will be paid when the insured dies.

For this example, there will be two classes, for two different life insurance product. The first, is the term life object. The TermLife class is shown in Listing 13.9

Listing 13.9: The TermLife Class (TermLife.java)

```
public class TermLife extends Policy implements
        Payable
{
   private String begin;
   private String end;

   public void setBegin(String s)
   {
        begin = s;
```

```
        }

        public String getBegin()
        {
                return begin;
        }


        public void setEnd(String s)
        {
                end = s;
        }

        public String getEnd()
        {
                return end;
        }

    public double getBenefit()
    {
                return(getFace());
    }
}
```

Term life insurance is a very simple, common type of life insurance. It is bought for a term, a number of years, and during that time period, if the insured dies, the face amount of the policy will be paid to the beneficiary. The additional attributes defined by this subclass of policy are shown in Table 13.3.

Table 13.3: Attributes of the TermLife Class

Property	Description
begin	The beginning date of the term that this policy is valid for.
end	The ending date of the term that this policy is valid for.

The term life class also implements the Payable interface. As a result it must include a getBenefit method. For term life, the benefit is always the face amount, and as a result, the getBenefit method returns the face amount.

In addition to term life, there is also whole life. Whole life insurance builds up a cash value over the life of the policy. This cash value is usually added to the death benefit. Listing 13.10 shows the whole life class.

Listing 13.10: The WholeLife Class (WholeLife.java)

```java
public class WholeLife extends Policy
  implements Payable
{
  private double cashValue;

  public double getCashValue()
  {
    return cashValue;
  }

  public void setCashValue(double d)
  {
    cashValue = d;
  }

  public double getBenefit()
  {
          return(getCashValue() + getFace());
  }
}
```

As you can see, the WholeLife class extends Policy and adds a cash-Value attribute. The getBenefit method returns the cash value plus the face amount.

Because both WholeLife and TermLife implement the payable interface, they can be used interchangeably by code that uses the Payable interface. Listing 13.11 shows a program that does this.

Listing 13.11: The insurance Application (InsuranceApp.java)

```java
public class InsuranceApp
{

  public static void main(String args[])
  {
    System.out.println("Insurance App");

    TermLife policy1 = new TermLife();
    policy1.setInsured("John Smith");
    policy1.setBeneficiary("Jeff Heaton");
    policy1.setFace(100000);
```

```
    WholeLife policy2 = new WholeLife();
    policy2.setInsured("Jane Smith");
    policy2.setBeneficiary("Jeff Heaton");
    policy2.setFace(100000);
    policy2.setCashValue(1000);

    cutCheck(policy1);
    cutCheck(policy2);

  }

  public static void cutCheck(Payable policy)
  {
        System.out.println(
          "The amount of:" + policy.getBenefit() );
  }
}
```

As you can see two policies are created named policy1 and policy2. Policy1 is a term life, whereas policy2 is whole life. A method is created named cutCheck, which could be used to write out a check for the amount the policy is payable for. Notice how cutCheck accepts an object of type Payable? This allows it to work with either the term or whole life policy. The method "cutCheck" is called for both policies and prints out the payable amount for each.

Chapter Review

In this chapter you were introduced to object oriented programming. Java is an object oriented language, so a basic understanding of object oriented programming is necessary to be effective with Java. This chapter only scratches the surface of object oriented programming. An entire book could easily be devoted to object oriented programming.

You saw that you can create your own classes. These classes can contain data. Data stored in classes should be accessible by getters and setters. The instance variables themselves should be private. You should implement a public get method to read the attribute, and a public set method to set the value of the attribute.

Classes can subclass other classes. When you subclass another class you inherit all of the other classes attributes and methods. The class that you subclassed becomes your parent class. Subclassing another class does not affect the parent class.

Exceptions are how Java reports errors. You can also create exceptions of your own. Exceptions are subclasses of the Exception class. Once you have created your own exception type, you can throw this exception when something goes wrong in your application. This allows you to communicate application specific error messages.

Interfaces allow you to publish common methods that your class supports. Any other class that supports this interface must have the interface methods. By guaranteeing all classes that implement this class will have the required methods, you can be sure that those classes will be supported as well.

New Terms

Child Class A child class is a class that inherits from a parent, or base, class. Has the same meaning as subclass.

Default Access When something has default access, other method's objects can access this method or variable if they are in the same package.

getter A getter is a public function used to access the value of a non-public class level variable.

interface An interface is like a class, except it only defines methods and functions. The methods and functions are only defined, not actually created. Then any class that implements the interface must also implement the methods and functions defined by the interface.

Parent Class A parent class has one, or more, subclasses.

private When something has private access, only methods in this class can access this variable or method.

protected When something has protected access, only subclasses of this object can access the variable or method.

public When something has public access, any other object's methods can access this variable or method.

setter A setter is a public method used to change the value of a non-public class level variable.

Subclass A subclass is a class that inherits from a parent, or base, class. Has the same meaning as child class.

Review Questions

1. Write the line of code that will declare an "int", named "i" that has default access.

2. Assume a parent and child class are in the same package. Does the child inherit from the parent, or does the parent inherit from the child?

3. When inheritance occurs in the same package, which access modifiers will be inherited?

4. Write the getters and setters for the following variable:

```
private int myVariable;
```

5. What is wrong with the following code?

```
interface MyInterface
{
   public int myfunction();
}

public class MyClass implements MyInterface
{
   public int myOtherFunction();
}
```

Assignment #11

Write a simple class that will hold a computer's record. You should store, the name of the computer, how many MEGs of RAM, how many GIGs on the hard drive, and the number of CD-ROM drives. Create this class and provide all necessary getters and setters.

CHAPTER 14: MORE OBJECT ORIENTED

In Chapter 14 you will learn about:
- **More Object Oriented Programming**
- **Using Objects in the Student List Example**

In this chapter we will build upon the last chapter by making use of the Student class. Many changes will be made to the StudentList class to make it object oriented. You will see how to take a non-object oriented program and turn it into an Object Oriented Program.

Updating the Student Class

To create this new program we will begin by creating a base class for the students. This base class will define a person, and the student class will become a child class of person. Let's look at the base class.

Base Class

The base class for Student is the Person class. The Person class used in this chapter is the same Person class used in Chapter 13. The person class, that we will create, is shown in Listing 14.1.

Listing 14.1: The Person Base Class (Person.java)

```java
public class Person
{
  private String first; // the person's first name
  private String last; // the person's last name

  public void setFirst(String theFirst)
  {
    first = theFirst;
  }

  public String getFirst()
  {
    return first;
  }

  public void setLast(String theLast)
  {
    last = theLast;
```

Learning Objective #1
Learn to create
a base class.

```
  }

  public String getLast()
  {
    return last;
  }
}
```

Now that the "Person" base class has been created, I will show you how to create the "Student" class. I will show you several versions of the "Student" class that take advantage of several of Java's object oriented features.

This is the same "Person" base class that was developed in Chapter 13. For more information on the "Person" class refer to Chapter 13.

Adding a toString Function

Learning Objective #2
Create a toString function.

One very handy feature of Java is the toString method. You can add a toString method to your own classes. This will allow your class to be printed using a single System.out.println. A toString method, is nothing more than a function you create, with the name "toString". However, naming it "toString", gives this function some special properties. Namely, it allows the object to represent itself as a string.

Listing 14.2 shows the Student class with a toString method.

Listing 14.2: Creating the Student Class (Student2.java)

```java
public class Student2 extends Person
{
  private int studentNumber;
  private String type;

  public void setStudentNumber(int theStudentNumber)
  {
    studentNumber = theStudentNumber;
  }

  public int getStudentNumber()
  {
    return studentNumber;
  }

  public void setType(String theType)
  throws TypeException
  {
    if( !theType.equalsIgnoreCase("Freshman") &&
        !theType.equalsIgnoreCase("Sophomore") &&
```

```
        !theType.equalsIgnoreCase("Junior") &&
        !theType.equalsIgnoreCase("Graduate") &&
        !theType.equalsIgnoreCase("Senior") )
      throw new TypeException(
        "Invalid type: must be Freshman, Sophomore, "
        +"Junior, Senior or Graduate");
    type = theType;
  }

  public String getType()
  {
    return type;
  }

  public String toString()
  {
    return(getLast() + ", " + getFirst() +
    ",student number: " + studentNumber + ", " +
    type );
  }
}
```

As you can see, the "toString" method returns a String in the form that you would want this object printed. For example, if you were to execute the following code.

```
Student2 student = new Student2();
student.setLast("Heaton");
student.setFirst("Jeff");
student.setType("Graduate");
student.setNumber(1001);
System.out.println(student);
```

The above code would print out:

```
Heaton, Jeff,student number:1001, Graduate
```

This is very handy, as you can print out the entire object with one System.out.println call.

If the toString function is NOT required, or if you do not provide a toString function a number, which corresponds to where your object is stored in memory, will be displayed.

A toString method would not be required for an object that has no way of being represented as a string. For example an object that holds a sound or an image, could not easily be represented as a String.

Adding a compareTo Function

Learning Objective #3
Create a compareTo function.

You can also implement a compareTo method. This will allow the student objects to be sorted. For this example, we want student objects to be sorted first by last name and secondly by first name. Adding a compareTo method will allow this to be done. Listing 14.3 shows the student class with a compareTo method. This is the final version of the Student class, which will be used in this book.

Listing 14.3: The Final Version of the Student Class (Student.java)

```java
public class Student extends Person
{
  private int studentNumber;
  private String type;

  public void setStudentNumber(int theStudentNumber)
  {
    studentNumber = theStudentNumber;
  }

  public int getStudentNumber()
  {
    return studentNumber;
  }

  public void setType(String theType)
  throws TypeException
  {
    if( !theType.equalsIgnoreCase("Freshman") &&
        !theType.equalsIgnoreCase("Sophomore") &&
        !theType.equalsIgnoreCase("Junior") &&
        !theType.equalsIgnoreCase("Graduate") &&
        !theType.equalsIgnoreCase("Senior") )
      throw new TypeException(
        "Invalid type: must be Freshman, Sophomore, "
        +" Junior, Senior or Graduate");
    type = theType;
  }

  public String getType()
  {
    return type;
  }
```

```
public String toString()
{
  return(getLast() + ", " + getFirst() +
  ",student number: " + studentNumber + ", " +
  type );
}

public int compareTo(Student student)
{
  int i = getLast().compareTo(student.getLast());
  if( i==0 )
    return getFirst().compareTo(student.getFirst());
  else
    return i;
}
}
```

Important
You are not required to include toString and compareTo functions in your programs, but it is usualy a good idea.

A compareTo method always compares the object itself, to the object passed in. For example, the following line of code compares "str1" to "str2".

```
if( str1.compareTo(str2) )
```

As you can see, the compareTo method first compares the last names. If the last names are the same, then the first names are compared. If the first and last names happen to be equal then the other object is considered to be the same, and the "compareTo" method will return 0. For more information on the return values of compareTo, see Chapter 10.

Integrating the Student Class

Now the student list example will be modified to use objects. This is not as big of a change as it might seem. The student list was previously made up of strings. Since the Student object can now be displayed like a string, because it has a toString method, much of the code remains the same.

The new StudentList example, which uses objects, is shown in Listing 14.3.

Listing 14.3: Creating a Student List (StudentList.java)

```
import java.io.*;

public class StudentList
{
  // used to read from the user
  static BufferedReader in;

  // how many students are there currently
```

```java
static int studentCount;

// the student list
static Student studentList[];

public static void bubbleSort(Student data[],
  int size)
{
  boolean done = false;
  int index;

  while (done == false)
  {
    done = true;
    for (index=1 ; index < size;index++)
    {
      if (data[index].compareTo(data[index-1])<0)
      {
        // swap data[index] and data[index-1]
        Student temp        = data[index];
        data[index]   = data[index-1];
        data[index-1] = temp;
        done = false;
      }
    }
  }
}


public static void addStudent()
{
  System.out.println("");
  System.out.println("*** Add Student ***");
  if( studentCount >24 )
  {
    System.out.println(
      "There are already 25 students, " +
      "which is the most you can have.");
    return;
  }

  System.out.print("Enter student's first name> ");
  String first = readInput();
  System.out.print("Enter student's last  name> ");
  String last = readInput();
  System.out.print(
```

```
        "Enter student's type(i.e.  Freshman> ");
    String type = readInput();
    System.out.print("Enter student's number> ");
    String n = readInput();

    Student student = new Student();

    try
    {
      int num = Integer.parseInt(n);
      student.setStudentNumber(num);
      student.setFirst(first);
      student.setLast(last);
      student.setType(type);
    }
    catch(NumberFormatException e)
    {
      System.out.println(
        "You did not enter a valid student number.");
      return;
    }
    catch(TypeException e)
    {
      System.out.println(e.getMessage());
      return;
    }

    studentList[studentCount] = student;
    studentCount = studentCount + 1;

    bubbleSort(studentList,studentCount);

  }

  public static void deleteStudent()
  {
    System.out.println("");
    System.out.println("*** Delete Student ***");
    if( studentCount == 0 )
    {
      System.out.println(
        "There are no students yet, no one to "+
        "delete.");
      return;
    }
```

```java
for(int i=0; i<studentCount; i++ )
{
  System.out.println( (i+1) + ":" +
    studentList[i] );
}

System.out.print(
  "Which student number do you wish to delete> ");
String str = readInput();
int number = 0;

try
{
  number = Integer.parseInt( str );
}
catch( NumberFormatException e)
{
  System.out.println(
    "You did not enter a valid number.");
  return;
}

if( number<1 )
{
  System.out.println(
    "Student number must be at least 1.");
  return;
}

if( number>studentCount )
{
  System.out.println(
    "Student number must be less than " +
    studentCount );
}

// now actually delete that student
int i = number-1;
while( i<studentCount )
{
  studentList[i] = studentList[i+1];
  i = i + 1;
}

studentCount = studentCount - 1;
```

```
}

public static void listStudents()
{
  System.out.println("");
  System.out.println("*** List Students ***");
  if( studentCount == 0 )
  {
    System.out.println(
      "There are no students yet.");
    return;
  }

  for(int i=0; i<studentCount; i++ )
  {
    System.out.println( studentList[i] );
  }
}

// a simple method that inputs a line
// from the user and returns it
public static String readInput()
{
  try
  {
    String input = in.readLine();
    input = input.trim();
    return input;
  }
  catch(IOException e)
  {
  }
  return "";// an error occured
}


public static void main(String args[])
{
  // setup the variables
  InputStreamReader inputStreamReader =
    new InputStreamReader ( System.in );
  in = new BufferedReader ( inputStreamReader );
  studentList = new Student[25];
  studentCount = 0;

  // now display the main menu
```

```java
        boolean done = false;

        while( done==false )
        {
          // print 25 blank lines to clear the screen
          for(int i=0;i<25;i++)
          {
            System.out.println("");
          }

          System.out.println(
            "*** Student List Main Menu ***");
          System.out.println("A> Add Student");
          System.out.println("D> Delete Student");
          System.out.println("L> List Students");
          System.out.println("Q> Quit program");
          System.out.print("Choose> ");

          // prompt the user
          String input = readInput();
          input = input.toUpperCase();
          char ch = input.charAt(0);
          switch( ch )
          {
            case 'A':
              addStudent();
              break;
            case 'D':
              deleteStudent();
              break;
            case 'L':
              listStudents();
              break;
            case 'Q':
              done = true;
              break;
            default:
              System.out.println(
                "Please choose a valid choice!");
          }
          System.out.println("");
          System.out.print("[Press any Enter/Return]");
          readInput();
        }
      }
    }
```

Now I will show you how each section of this program functions. I will begin with the "main" method.

The Main Method

The main method does two things. First it sets up the static instance variables, and secondly it performs the main loop. In this section we will examine how the static instance variables and the main loop are setup.

The main method begins with the following lines:

```
// setup the variables
InputStreamReader inputStreamReader =
   new InputStreamReader ( System.in );
in = new BufferedReader ( inputStreamReader );
studentList = new Student[25];
studentCount = 0;
```

First the input stream is setup. This is the same for any program that requires user input, except that the "in" variable is now a static instance variable, in this example. This allows it to be accessed anywhere in the program. If you need to review reading from the user, refer to Chapter 4.

Next the studentList variable is set to an array of size 25 Student objects. Finally, the student count is set to zero. The studentCount variable will always contain the number of students

The Main Loop

The main loop of the program displays the main menu and prompts the user for which option they would like to perform. The main loop begins with the following lines of code.

```
// now display the main menu
boolean done = false;

while( done==false )
{
  // print 25 blank lines to clear the screen
  for(int i=0;i<25;i++)
  {
    System.out.println("");
  }
```

First, a while loop is started with the "done" variable. The while loop will continue so long as the "done" variable is false, which is was just set to. The program will loop, displaying the main menu, until done is false. This allows the program to keep running after the user has chosen one of the main menu options. Once the user finally chooses Quit, the done variable will be set to true, and the program will terminate.

The main loop also displays 25 blank lines. This clears off anything that was previously on the screen, and makes the main menu more clear.

Next the program displays the main menu to the user and prompts for a choice, as seen here.

```
System.out.println("*** Student List Main Menu ***");
System.out.println("A> Add Student");
System.out.println("D> Delete Student");
System.out.println("L> List Students");
System.out.println("Q> Quit program");
System.out.print("Choose> ");

// prompt the user
String input = readInput();
input = input.toUpperCase();
char ch = input.charAt(0);
switch( ch )
{
  case 'A':
    addStudent();
    break;
  case 'D':
    deleteStudent();
    break;
```

First the main menu is displayed. Then the user is prompted for a line of text. That line of text is converted to uppercase, otherwise we would have to compare against both 'A' and 'a' for add user. Next, we use a switch/case to decide which option the user wants to do. Each of the menu options has a method that carries it out. The switch case decides which method needs to be called.

Adding a Student

To add a student, a new Student object is created and then added to the list. The add a student method begins as shown here:

```
System.out.println("");
System.out.println("*** Add Student ***");
if( studentCount >24 )
{
  System.out.println(
    "There are already 25 students, " +
    "which is the most you can have.");
  return;
}

System.out.print("Enter student's first name> ");
String first = readInput();
System.out.print("Enter student's last  name> ");
String last - readInput();
System.out.print(
  "Enter student's type(i.e.  Freshman> ");
String type = readInput();
System.out.print("Enter student's number> ");
String n = readInput();
```

First the method checks to see if there are already 25 students. If there are, an error is displayed, and the method returns. Then the program prompts the user for the first and last name of the student. The user is also prompted for the student type and number. No validation is done yet. Eventually the program will validate to ensure that proper first and last names, as well as student numbers were entered.

Next, a Student object is created.

```
Student student = new Student();

try
{
  int num = Integer.parseInt(n);
  student.setStudentNumber(num);
  student.setFirst(first);
  student.setLast(last);
  student.setType(type);
}
catch(NumberFormatException e)
{
  System.out.println(
    "You did not enter a valid student number.");
  return;
}
```

```
catch(TypeException e)
{
  System.out.println(e.getMessage());
  return;
}
```

The student number is converted from a string to an int. If this is an invalid number, then the exception is caught and an error message is printed. The rest of the attributes of the student object are set and if an invalid type is chosen, an exception is thrown and an error message displayed.

Once the student object has been setup, it is added to the list of students.

```
studentList[studentCount] = student;
studentCount = studentCount + 1;

bubbleSort(studentList,studentCount);
```

The student is added to the last array element, pointed to by studentCount. Next, studentCount is increased by one. Finally, bubbleSort is called to reorder the list. The bubbleSort method works just as it does before, only it uses Student objects rather than Strings. And because Student objects have a compareTo, just like String, the ONLY change require was changing all of the String objects to Student objects.

Deleting a Student

Deleting a student is somewhat more complex. This is done in several parts:

- Display a list of all students
- Prompt user for which student to delete
- Make sure the user entered a valid student
- Actually delete the student

To display a list of all students the following code is used:

```
System.out.println("");
System.out.println("*** Delete Student ***");
```

```
if( studentCount == 0 )
{
  System.out.println(
    "There are no students yet, "+
    "no one to delete.");
  return;
}

for(int i=0; i<studentCount; i++ )
{
  System.out.println( (i+1) + ":" +
    studentList[i] );
}
```

First, a check is performed to see if there are any students. If there are no students, then there is nothing to display. If this is the case, the program will exit with an error message.

Next, the program loops through all students and displays each student, with a student number. The student number is the array index of that student plus one. We add one to the student number so that there is no student with the student number of zero. This is done mainly for looks. People are used to seeing lists that start with one, not zero.

Then, the method prompts the user for the student number to delete and validates that student number.

```
System.out.print("Which student number do you wish to
delete> ");
String str = readInput();
int number = 0;

try
{
  number = Integer.parseInt( str );
}
catch( NumberFormatException e)
{
  System.out.println(
    "You did not enter a valid number.");
  return;
}

if( number<1 )
{
```

```
  System.out.println(
    "Student number must be at least 1.");
  return;
}

if( number>studentCount )
{
  System.out.println(
    "Student number must be less than "
    + studentCount );
}
```

As you can see, the student number is first read in as a string. This string is then converted to an int. The NumberFormat exception is caught, just in case the user enters an invalid number. The number is checked to see if it is below 1 or above the total number of students. Either of these is an error and causes the method to return.

Finally, we actually delete the student. This is done with the following lines of code.

```
// now actually delete that student
int i = number-1;
while( i<studentCount )
{
  studentList[i] = studentList[i+1];
  i = i + 1;
}

studentCount = studentCount - 1;
```

Let me explain how this deletes a user (to see a more visual description refer back to Chapter 11). The variable "i" is assigned to the array element that you want to delete. Remember, we added one to every array element to show the user, so we need to subtract one to balance that. If the user said to delete student 1, the first student, that is really array element 0, the first array element.

Listing the Students

The last operation that we will examine is listing the students. This is probably the simplest of the operations. The listStudents method is shown here.

```
public static void listStudents()
{
  System.out.println("");
  System.out.println("*** List Students ***");
  if( studentCount == 0 )
  {
    System.out.println(
      "There are no students yet.");
    return;
  }

  for(int i=0; i<studentCount; i++ )
  {
    System.out.println( studentList[i] );
  }
}
```

This method begins by checking to see if there are any students. If there are none, that is displayed and the method exits. Next, the method loops over the entire array and displays each student. The students are displayed in the order they were added.

The data for each student is displayed by using the "toString" function that was created earlier for the "Student" class. As you can see, the students are displayed simply by passing each student object, which is an array element, to the "println" method. As previously discussed, this automatically calls the "toString" function.

Chapter Review

In this chapter we modified the student list example to use objects. This required some changes to both the Student class and the StudentList class as well. The Student class was enhanced to include both a toString and compareTo method. The "toString" method allows the student object to be quickly converted to a string for printing. The compareTo method compares this Student object to another object to determine which one comes first alphabetically. In the case of the Student class, we sort first by last name, and secondly, by first name.

New Terms

compareTo A function, which the programmer can optionally provide, that is used to compare the class to another class.

toString A function, which the programmer can optionally provide, that is used to convert the object into a String.

Review Questions

1. Briefly describe what the purpose of the toString function is.

2. Briefly describe what the purpose of the compareTo function is.

3. What is the connection between the bubble sort and the compareTo function?

4. Is it REQUIRED that each class that you create contain both a toString and compareTo function?

5. What is printed out for an object that has no toString function?

Assignment #12

Extend the computer class that you created in Assignment #12. You should extend the class to include a toString and a compareTo function. The toString function should print out all information on the computer. The compareTo function should compare two computer's names.

CHAPTER 15: GUI PROGRAMMING

In Chapter 15 you will learn about:
- **What is Swing?**
- **Java GUI Applications**
- **Displaying Data to the User**
- **Reading Data from the User**

So far our applications have been text only. In this chapter you will see how to interact with the user with windows.

Java GUI Applications

So far we have only seen text based console applications. However, most of the applications that you use everyday are not text based console applications. Most applications these days are GUI applications. GUI stands for Graphical User Interface. By GUI applications I mean that they take advantage of such visual items as:

- Menu Bars
- Multiple Windows
- Icons
- Toolbars
- Multi-Font Display

Java is quite capable of creating these types of applications. In this book I will show you only the beginnings of how to create such applications.

To create a GUI application you must use a part of Java called Swing.

What is Swing

Swing allows Java to create graphical applications. Swing applications can use all of the graphical elements that make up most applications today. Figure 15.1 shows a Swing application written in Java.

Figure 15.1: A Swing Application

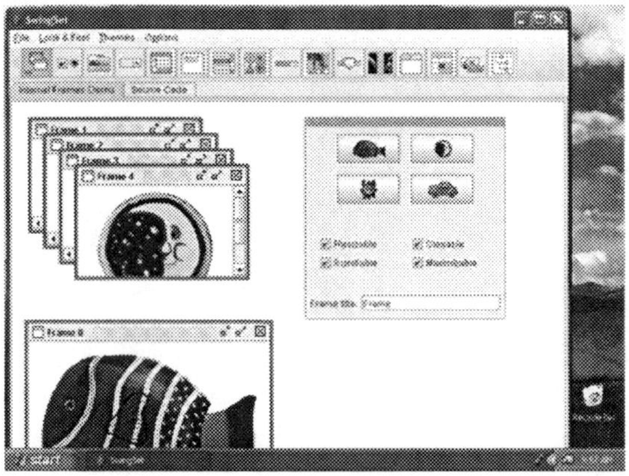

This application makes use of many features in Swing. As you can see this application contains many of the features you would normally see in a Windows application.

Using Swing

In this book you will learn to use Swing. I will focus on the dialog boxes provided by JOptionPane. These dialog boxes can be broken up into four groups.

- Confirmation Dialog Boxes
- Input Dialog Boxes
- Message Dialog Boxes
- Option Dialog Boxes

Confirmation dialog boxes ask the user to confirm things, in a yes/no fashion. For example, "Delete the file yes/no". Input dialog boxes prompt the user for a line of text. Message Dialog Boxes are used to display information to the user. Option Dialog Boxes combine features of the previous three dialog box types.

I will now show you how each of these dialog box types work.

Learning Objective #1
Learn to use
message dialogs.

Using Message Dialog Boxes

Message Dialog Boxes are used to present information to the user. Figure 15.2 shows a simple Message Dialog Box.

Figure 15.2: A Message Dialog Box

Creating a Message Dialog Box is very easy. Listing 15.1 shows the program used to create the Message Dialog Box shown in Figure 15.2.

Listing 15.1: Creating a Message Dialog Box (MessageDialog.java)

```
import javax.swing.*;

public class MessageDialog
{
  public static void main(String args[])
  {
    JOptionPane.showMessageDialog(
      null,
      "Hello World",
      "My Swing Application",
      JOptionPane.ERROR_MESSAGE);
  }
}
```

As you can see, the Message Dialog Box is displayed using the JOptionPane.showMessageDialog method. There are four parameters that are passed to this method. The first, which is null in this case, specifies the parent window of this message box. For this book, this parameter will always be null. The next parameter, "Hello World," specifies the text that will be displayed for this dialog box. The third parameter, "My Swing Application," specifies the title of the dialog box. The fourth parameter specifies what icon will be displayed. In this case we are using the ERROR_MESSAGE icon. You can choose from any of the following:

- ERROR_MESSAGE
- INFORMATION_MESSAGE
- WARNING_MESSAGE
- QUESTION_MESSAGE
- PLAIN_MESSAGE

By specifying different icon types you can customize the look of the dialog box to suit the purpose it is being used for.

Using Confirm Dialog Boxes

The dialog box used in the last section can display data to the user. However, the user can not interact with the dialog box in any way. The user simply clicks "OK" and the dialog box goes away. Confirm Dialog Boxes allow a limited degree of interactivity with the user. Figure 15.3 shows a Confirm Dialog Box.

Figure 15.3: A Confirm Dialog Box

Learning Objective #2
Learn to use
confirm dialogs.

As you can see, this dialog box contains more than one button. The user is allowed to click either the "Yes" or "No" button. Using a Confirm Dialog Box you can quickly prompt the user for yes/no questions. The code used to produce Figure 15.3 is shown in Listing 15.2.

Listing 15.2: A Confirm Dialog Box (ConfirmDialog.java)

```java
import javax.swing.*;

public class ConfirmDialog
{
  public static void main(String args[])
  {
    int i = JOptionPane.showConfirmDialog(null,
      "Do you like the color red?",
      "My Swing Application",
      JOptionPane.YES_NO_OPTION);

    if( i==JOptionPane.YES_OPTION )
    {
      JOptionPane.showMessageDialog(
        null,
        "Good, I like it too!",
        "My Swing Application",
        JOptionPane.ERROR_MESSAGE);
    }
    else
    {
      JOptionPane.showMessageDialog(
```

```
            null,
            "Why? It is a very nice color!",
            "My Swing Application",
            JOptionPane.ERROR_MESSAGE);
    }
  }
}
```

Confirm Dialog Boxes are good for when you do not need to input any textual data from the user. You just need to ask a yes/no question. In the next section we will see how you can use Input Dialog Boxes to prompt the user for information.

Using Input Dialogs

We already saw that console programs can input a line of text. Inputting a single line of text from the user with a Swing application can be done with an Input Dialog Box. Input Dialog Boxes display a line to tell the user what to enter, then an OK and Cancel button. Figure 15.4 shows a simple Input Dialog Box.

Figure 15.4: An Input Dialog Box

Learning Objective #3
Learn to use
input dialogs.

As you can see, the Input Dialog Box can prompt the user to input text information. Just like any string, if you want numeric information, convert the string to a number using Integer.parseInt, or a similar function. Listing 15.3 shows the Java code used to create this dialog box.

Listing 15.3: An input Dialog Box (InputDialog.java)

```
import javax.swing.*;

public class InputDialog
{
  public static void main(String args[])
  {
    String name = JOptionPane.showInputDialog(null,
      "Please enter your name?",
```

Java for the Beginning Programmer

```
              "My Swing Application",
              JOptionPane.QUESTION_MESSAGE);

          JOptionPane.showMessageDialog(
             null,
             "Hello " + name,
             "My Swing Application",
             JOptionPane.INFORMATION_MESSAGE);
      }
  }
```

Important
Input dialogs will
return null if the
user clicks cancel.

As you can see the showMessageDialog method accepts four parameters. The first specifies the parent window, since there is none, we pass in null. The second is the prompt to display. The third is the title of the dialog box. The third is the icon to display. You can chose from any of the icon types previously mentioned.

The string that the user entered is returned. For this program we display the name that the user entered.

Another important point of the Input Dialog Box is what happens when the user clicks the cancel button. If the user clicks the cancel button than "null" is returned for the string. Because of this it is very important to check for "null" when the Input Dialog Box returns.

Using Option Dialog Boxes

Learning Objective #4
Learn to use
option dialogs.

We have already seen the Confirm Dialog Box that allows you to ask the user Yes/No questions. What happens if you have more answers than just Yes/No. If you need more answers, you can use the Option Dialog Box. Figure 15.6 shows an Option Dialog Box.

Figure 15.5: An Option Dialog Box

As you can see the above dialog box looks very similar to the Confirm Dialog Box. The main difference is that rather than just having "Yes" and "No", you can choose from additional options such as "Red", "Green", etc. Option Dialog Boxes allow you to specify what the answers are. Listing 15.4 shows the Java code that was used to produce the above Option Dialog Box.

Listing 15.4: An Option Dialog (OptionDialog.java)

```java
import javax.swing.*;

public class OptionDialog
{
  public static void main(String args[])
  {

    Object[] options = { "Red", "Green", "Blue", "Other" };

    int color = JOptionPane.showOptionDialog(
      null,
      "What is your favorite color?",
      "My Swing Application",
      JOptionPane.DEFAULT_OPTION,
      JOptionPane.QUESTION_MESSAGE,
      null,
      options,
      options[0]);

    JOptionPane.showMessageDialog(
        null,
        "You entered " + options[color],
        "My Swing Application",
        JOptionPane.INFORMATION_MESSAGE);
  }
}
```

As shown above, the showOptionDialog method accepts eight parameters. These additional parameters allow the programmer to control its appearance. The first parameter specifies the parent window, since there is no parent window, this parameter is null. The second parameter specifies the prompt that is to be displayed to the user. This tells the user what they are entering. The third parameter specifies he name of the application. The fourth specifies options for the option box. The fifth parameter specifies the icon type to be used, which uses the same options as already shown in previous dialog boxes. The sixth parameter specifies a custom icon to use.

There is none, so we provide a null. This parameter accepts any Java Icon object. The seventh parameter specifies the list of options, which is an array of strings. The eight parameter specifies which of the options should be the default option.

Chapter Review

In this chapter you learned how to create graphical applications. Java provides common dialog boxes that you can use for common functions. Java's common dialog boxes are the message, confirm, input and Option Dialog Box. The Message Dialog Box displays messages to the user. The Confirm Dialog Box asks the user a yes/no question. The Input Dialog Box allows the user to enter a line of text. The Option Dialog Box allows the user to select from a predefined set of choices.

New Terms

GUI Graphical User Interface (GUI) applications use windows, menus and other graphical elements to communicate with the user.

Confirm Dialog Box A Confirm Dialog Box prompts the user with Yes/No or Yes/No/Cancel options.

Input Dialog Box An Input Dialog Box allows the user to enter text.

Message Dialog Box A Message Dialog Box displays a message to the user.

Option Dialog Box An Option Dialog Box presents the user with several options.

Swing Swing is a set of classes that Java makes available to the user to implement GUI applications.

Review Questions

1. Describe what a Confirm Dialog Box might be used for.

2. Describe what an Input Dialog Box might be used for.

3. Describe what a Message Dialog Box might be used for.

4. Describe what an Option Dialog Box might be used for.

5. What is happens if the user clicks cancel for the Input Dialog Box?

Assignment #13

Write a simple program, named Assignment14, that will prompt the user for
the length and width of a rectangle. Display the area of that rectangle. This
application should be implemented as a GUI application.

CHAPTER 16: FINAL EXAM

Chapter 16 contains an example Final Exam. Some questions will have more than one correct answer. Appendix B contains the answers, and a review of the correct answer.

1. A while loop will execute at least once?

A>   True

B>   False

2. Which of the following commands is used to run a Java application?

A>   run

B>   javac

C>   java

D>   execute

3. You would like to use Java to display a chart on a website. What do you use?

A>   Console Application

B>   GUI Application

C>   Java Applet

4. Which of the following Java data types could be used to hold the number 3.5? (more than one may be correct)

A>   float

B>   double

C>   int

5. How do you compare stra to strb, assuming both are strings?

A>   if(stra==strb)

B>   if(stra.equals(strb))

C>   if(stra = strb)

6. A switch/case is often used to replace an if/else ladder.

A>   True

B>   False

7. Which of the following would you most likely store inside of a String?

A> The name of your father.

B> The year that a person was born.

C> The price of butter.

8. Which of the following variable types can not hold decimal places? (i.e. 3.31). (more than one may be correct)

A> byte

B> short

C> int

D> long

E> float

F> double

9. What numbers would the following loop count through?

```
for(int i=0;i<10;i++)
```

A>   0,1,2,3,4,5,6,7,8,9,10

B>   1,2,3,4,5,6,7,8,9,10

C>   0,1,2,3,4,5,6,7,8,9

D>   1,2,3,4,5,6,7,8,9

10. What happens when an Exception occurs inside of a try block, and there is a catch block that handles this sort of exception?

A>   The program terminates(crashes)

B>   An error message is displayed and the program continues.

C>   The program executes the catch block.

11. Which index item(i.e. array[index item]) do arrays start with?

A>   0

B>   1

C>   double

12. How do you know when a bubble sort is done?

A> It is done when you reach the last element of an array

B> It is done when it finds the first pair of elements that does not need to be swapped.

C> It is done when it makes it through the array with no swaps.

13. What is true of instance variables in properly written Object Oriented Program (OOP) programs?

A> They should be only accessed through getters/setters

B> Nothing is wrong with public variables.

C> Public variables are okay, but you must make them static as well.

14. What would be the output of the following?

```
String str="Java";
System.out.println( str.charAt(0) );
```

A> Nothing, it would throw an out of bounds error.

B> J

C> a

15. How far would the following loop count?

```
for(int i=1;i<10;i++)
```

A>   0 to 10.

B>   From 1 to 9.

C>   From 0 to 9.

16. What does the Java import statement do?

A>   Displays a line of text.

B>   Not a valid Java statement.

C>   Allows your program to use other classes.

17. Are Java variable names case sensitive?

A>   Yes.

B>   No.

18. What is the output of the following?

```
String str = "Java";
System.out.println( str.length() );
```

A> 1

B> 2

C> 3

D> 4

E> Nothing, an exception would be thrown.

19. Which of the following makes use of Java's single-line comment?

A>

Comment line 1

#comment line 2

B>

// Comment line 1

// Comment line 2

C>

– Comment line 1

– Comment line 2

D>

/* Comment line 1

Comment line 2 */

20. How do you create an array of 10 int's?

A>   int x[] = new int[10];

B>   int x() = new int(10);

C>   int x[10];

21. Is the following code correct (i.e. will not throw an exception)?

```
int x[];
x = new int[10];
x[10] = 5;
```

A> Yes.

B> No.

22. What happens when you pass a bad number (i.e. "33jj2") to the Integer. parseInt method?

A> A NumberFormatException is thrown.

B> The method would return 0.

C> The method would return -1.

D> The method would return null.

23. If the variable str contains a string and the variable d contains a double, how do you convert str into a double?

A> d = str;

B> d = val(str);

C> d = Double.parseDouble(str);

Java for the Beginning Programmer

24. What is the purpose of the substr method of the String class?

A>   It subtracts a string.

B>   It gets the length of the string.

C>   It can be used to break the string into smaller pieces

25. How large is the following array? String str[15]

A>   Not valid, you don't declare a string in Java with a length.

B>   15

C>   14

GLOSSARY

.class A file type that holds a compiled Java program/class. (Chapter 2)

.java A file type that holds the source code for a Java program/class. (Chapter 2)

A

Applet A Java application that runs from within a web browser. (Chapter 1)

array An array is a list of objects or primitive datatypes. Arrays start at index zero. (Chapter 11)

B

boolean A primitive datatype that holds true or false. (Chapter 3)

Boolean class A holder class for the boolean primitive datatype. (Chapter 3)

break If a break is placed inside of a case statement, the execution for that case statement ends. If a break is placed inside of a loop, the loop terminates. (Chapter 9)

Bubble Sort A bubble sort is a method by which a list of items can be sorted. The bubble sort swaps pairs of items until the list is sorted. (Chapter 12)

BufferedStreamReader A Java class that is used to read data from a device. For this book, it is used only to read data from the keyboard. (Chapter 4)

By Reference Variables can be passed to methods and functions "by reference". If this is the case, then changes made to the argument in the method will remain after the method terminates. (Chapter 6)

By Value Variables can be passed to methods and functions "by value". If this is the case, a copy of the variable is passed to the method or function, this then changes made to the argument in the method will not remain after the method terminates. (Chapter 6)

byte A Java primitive data type that holds very small numbers that would fit into a single byte. (Chapter 3)

Byte class A holder class for the byte primitive datatype. (Chapter 3)

C

case A case statement occurs inside of a switch statement. There is one case statement for each decision that the switch/case will make. (Chapter 5)

catch The catch-block allows the Java program to handle its own errors, and not simply terminate when an exception happens. When an exception occurs inside of a try-block, the code inside of the catch-block is executed to handle that error. (Chapter 4)

char A primitive data type that holds single characters. To hold multiple characters, see the String class. (Chapter 3)

Character A character is the building block of the String. Individual characters, which usually correspond to keys on the keyboard, make up strings. (Chapter 10)

charAt The charAt function is a part of the String class. It is used to obtain an individual character inside of a string. (Chapter 10)

Child Class A child class is a class that inherits from a parent, or base, class. Has the same meaning as subclass. (Chapter 13)

Class A class is an object data type provided by Java or the program. (Chapter 6)

Comment A note that is placed in the program by the programmer. The comment has no effect on the way that the program runs. Comments can be single line or multi-line. (Chapter 3)

compareTo The compareTo function is a part of the String class. It determines the placement of two strings. For example, strA.compareTo(strB) would return 0 if the two strings are equal, a number less than 0, if strA comes before strB. Or a number greater than 0, if strB comes before strA. (Chapter 12)

Compile When java source code is compiled into a form that the computer can easily understand. This converts a .java file into a .class file. (Chapter 2)

Confirm Dialog Box A confirm dialog box prompts the user with Yes/No or Yes/No/Cancel options. (Chapter 15)

Console Application A Java application that can only display text. (Chapter 1)

Constant A variable that holds a fixed value and cannot be changed. Java constants always start with the keyword final. (Chapter 3)

continue The continue statement causes the current loop to jump back to the top of the loop, without processing the rest of the code in the loop's body. (Chapter 9)

crash When a program stops in an unplanned manner. Usually the crash is the result of an exception that was not caught. (Chapter 4)

Cross Platform The ability for a program to run on more than one type of computer system. (Chapter 1)

D

Declare A variable, or array, is declared when its name and type are given. For example int i declares a variable of type "int", named "i". (Chapter 11)

default If none of the case statements are executed, and a default statement is provided, the default statement will be executed. (Chapter 5)

Default Access When something has default access, other method's objects can access this method or variable if they are in the same package. (Chapter 13)

Do/While Loop The do/while loop is one of Java's three loop types. The do/while loop will execute its body one or more times so long as a condition is true. The main difference between the while and do/while loops is that the do/while is guaranteed to execute at least once. (Chapter 9)

double A Java primitive datatype that can hold floating point numbers. The double datatype is larger than the float datatype. (Chapter 3)

Double class A holder class for the double primitive datatype. (Chapter 3)

E

else The else statement works with the if statement. If the if statement does not execute, then the else statement will be executed. (Chapter 5)

equals The equals method can be used to compare two strings. For example str.equals("Java") compares str to "Java". (Chapter 5)

equalsIgnoreCase The equalsIgnoreCase method can be used to compare two strings, without regard to case. For example str.equalsIgnoreCase("Java") compares str to "Java," "JaVa" etc. (Chapter 5)

Exception An exception occurs in Java when an error occurs. Exceptions, if not caught, will cause the program to crash. (Chapter 4)

Execute When your Java program begins execution. Execute has the same meaning as run. (Chapter 2)

F

final The Java keyword that designates a variable as constant. (Chapter 3)

float A Java primitive data type that holds floating point numbers. The float datatype is smaller than the double datatype. (Chapter 3)

Float class A holder class for the float primitive datatype. (Chapter 3)

For Loop The for loop is one of Java's three loop types. The for loop will execute its body over a range of values, so long as a condition is true. The for loop may execute zero times, if its condition is is not true. (Chapter 9)

Function A reusable block of code that can be called from elsewhere in the program. A function returns a value. (Chapter 6)

G

getter A getter is a public function used to access the value of a non-public class level variable. (Chapter 13)

GUI Graphical User Interface (GUI) applications use windows, menus and other graphical elements to communicate with the user. (Chapter 15)

GUI Application A Java application that uses Windows and the mouse. (Chapter 1)

H,I

if The if statement allows Java to make decisions and compare variables. (Chapter 5)

if/else Ladder A series of if/else statements together is called a if/else ladder. If/else ladders are often replaced with switch/case statements. (Chapter 5)

indent Java source code is indented to make it appear clearer. (Chapter 3)

index An index is a number that references a character position or array element. Both character positions and array elements start at index zero. (Chapter 11)

indexOf The indexOf function is a part of the String class. It is used to search the string for substrings or characters. (Chapter 10)

Initialize An array or object is initialized when it is assigned a value. An array must be instantiated before it can be initialized. (Chapter 11)

Input Dialog Box An input dialog box allows the user to enter text. (Chapter 15)

InputStreamReader A Java class that is used to read data from a device. For this book, it is used only to read data from the keyboard. (Chapter 4)

Instance Function A function that is not declared static. To access an instance function the class must have been instantiated with the "new" operator. (Chapter 6)

Instance Method A method that is not declared static. To access an instance function the class must have been instantiated with the "new" operator. (Chapter 6)

Instance Variable A variable that is not declared static. To access an instance variable the class must have been instantiated with the "new" operator. (Chapter 6)

Instantiate An array or object is instantiated when the object is actually allocated using the "new" operator. An array or object must be declared before it can be instantiated. (Chapter 11)

int A Java primitive datatype used to hold numbers. The int datatype is smaller than the long datatype, but larger than the short datatype. (Chapter 3)

Integer class A holder class for the integer primitive datatype. (Chapter 3)

interface An interface is like a class, except it only defines methods and functions. The methods and functions are only defined, not actually created. Then any class that implements the interface must also implement the methods and functions defined by the interface. (Chapter 13)

J

java The command to execute/run a Java application. (Chapter 2)

javac The command to compile a Java application. (Chapter 2)

K,L

length The length function is a part of the String class. It is used to obtain the length of a string. (Chapter 10)

Local Variable A variable that is local to a method or function. Any value assigned to the variable only has meaning in the method, and will lose its value when the method returns. (Chapter 6)

long A Java primitive datatype used to hold numbers. The long datatype is larger than the int datatype. (Chapter 3)

Long class A holder class for the long primitive datatype. (Chapter 3)

Loop A loop is a block of code that is executed until a condition is no longer true. (Chapter 9)

M

Message Dialog Box A message dialog box displays a message to the user. (Chapter 15)

Method A reusable block of code that can be called from elsewhere in the program. A method does not return a value. (Chapter 6)

N

Nested Loop A nested loop is a loop that is placed inside of another loop. (Chapter 9)

NumberFormatException An exception that occurs when a non-number string is passed to one of the parse functions. For example, the string "182g" would produce this exception if used with Integer.parseInt. (Chapter 4)

Numeric Datatype A datatype that holds numbers, and can have mathematical operations performed on it. (Chapter 4)

O

Object An instance of a class. (Chapter 6)

Option Dialog Box An option dialog box presents the user with several options. (Chapter 15)

P

Parent Class A parent class has one, or more, subclasses. (Chapter 13)

Parse Parsing is the process where the computer processes a string and converts it into a form that the computer can understand. For example, parsing a telephone number would likely involve removing any hyphen and parenthesis characters form the string and leaving only digits. (Chapter 10)

Primitive Data Type A datatype that is not a class. Java's primitive datatypes are: char, byte, short, int, long, float, double and boolean. (Chapter 3)

print A Java method that will display a line of text, but not move to the next line. (Chapter 4)

println A Java method that will display a line of text, and will move to the next line. (Chapter 4)

private When something has private access only methods in this class can access this variable or method. (Chapter 13)

protected When something has protected access only subclasses of this object can access the variable or method. (Chapter 13)

public When something has public access any other object's methods can access this variable or method. (Chapter 13)

R,S

readLine A Java method that prompts the user to enter a line of text. The user is allowed to enter text until the user presses the ENTER key. (Chapter 4)

setter A setter is a public method used to change the value of a non-public class level variable. (Chapter 13)

short A Java primitive datatype that holds numbers. The short datatype is smaller than the int datatype. (Chapter 3)

Short class A holder class for the short primitive datatype. (Chapter 3)

Source Code The instructions that a programmer enters to create an application. (Chapter 1)

static A Java keyword that can be applied to a variable, method, function or other Java construct. See "Static Function", "Static Method", or "Static Variable". (Chapter 6)

Static Function A function that is declared static. A static function can be accessed either through an instance or directly through the class. (Chapter 6)

Static Method A method that is declared static. A static function can be accessed either through an instance or directly through the class. (Chapter 6)

Static Variable A variable that is declared static. A static variable can be accessed either through an instance or directly through the class, if it is declared at the class level. If the static variable is declared in a function or method, then it will hold its value, even after the method terminates. (Chapter 6)

String A String is a Java datatype that holds text information. A String is made up of individual characters. (Chapter 10)

String Datatype A datatype that holds text information. You cannot preform mathematical operations on the String. (Chapter 4)

Subclass A subclass is a class that inherits from a parent, or base, class. Subclass has the same meaning as child class. (Chapter 13)

substr The substr function is a part the String class. It is used to break the string into smaller "substrings". (Chapter 10)

Swap A swap occurs when the contents of two variables must be exchanged. To properly swap two variables, a third, temporary variable is needed. (Chapter 12)

Swing is a set of classes that Java makes available to the user to implement GUI applications. (Chapter 15)

switch Used to compare a variable to any of the provided case statements. If no case statement matches, the default statement(if provided) will be executed. (Chapter 5)

System A Java class that provides many important methods and variables for interacting with the computer system. (Chapter 4)

System.in The standard input. This variable is used to receive keyboard input from the user. (Chapter 4)

System.out The standard output. This variable is used to display data on the console. (Chapter 4)

T

Temporary Variable A temporary variable is a variable that is used as a place holder for something for a very short time. A temporary variable is almost always a local variable. (Chapter 12)

toString A programmer can provide a toString method, which is used to convert the object to a String. This allows an object, such as "obj" to be printed to the screen using a simple System.out.println call. (Chapter 12)

try The try-block encloses code that might cause an exception. If an exception does happen in a try block, the try block's catch-block is execute. (Chapter 4)

Type Cast To convert from one datatype to another. A cast is usually denoted by the desired datatype in parenthesis, such as (int). (Chapter 3)

U,V,W,X,Y,Z

While Loop The while loop is one of Java's three loop types. The while loop will execute its body one or more times so long as a condition is true. The main difference between the while and do/while loops is that the while is not guaranteed to execute at least once. (Chapter 9)

APPENDIX A: DOWNLOADING EXAMPLES

This book contains many source code examples. You do not need to retype any of these examples, they all can be downloaded from the Internet. Simply go to the site:

http://www.heatonresearch.com/download/

This site will give you more information on how to download the example programs.

APPENDIX B: FINAL EXAM ANSWERS

1. A while loop will execute at least once?

    A> True

    B> False

Correct answer: B
The only loop that will execute at least once is the do/while loop. The for or while loop may execute zero times if the condition is not initially true.

2. Which of the following commands is used to run a Java application?

    A> run

    B> javac

    C> java

    D> execute

Correct answer: C

The java command will run a Java program. The javac command will compile a Java program. The run and execute commands do not exist for Java.

3. You would like to use Java to display a chart on a website. What do you use?

A>   Console Application

B>   GUI Application

C>   Java Applet

Correct answer: C

Because this application is going to be run from the web, an applet is best. Otherwise, if not for the web, a GUI application would have been used.

4. Which of the following Java data types could be used to hold the number 3.5? (more than one may be correct)

A>   float

B>   double

C>   int

Correct answers: A, B

The datatypes float and double are the only datatypes listed that support floating point.

5. How do you compare stra to strb, assuming both are strings?

A> if(stra==strb)

B> if(stra.equals(strb))

C> if(stra = strb)

Correct answer: B

Never use = or == to compare two strings

6. A switch/case is often used to replace an if/else ladder.

A> True

B> False

Correct answer: A

Switch/case can often be used to replace a if/else ladder, for integer values.

7. Which of the following would you most likely store inside of a String?

A> The name of your father.

B> The year that a person was born.

C> The price of butter.

Correct answer: A

Strings are used to store text, which the name of your father would be.

302 Java for the Beginning Programmer

8. Which of the following variable types can not hold decimal places? (i.e. 3.31).(more than one may be correct)

    A> byte

    B> short

    C> int

    D> long

    E> float

    F> double

Correct answer: A, B, C, D

Of the listed datatypes only float and double allow decimal places.

9. What numbers would the following loop count through?

```
for(int i=0;i<10;i++)
```

    A> 0,1,2,3,4,5,6,7,8,9,10

    B> 1,2,3,4,5,6,7,8,9,10

    C> 0,1,2,3,4,5,6,7,8,9

    D> 1,2,3,4,5,6,7,8,9

Correct answer: C

This loop starts at zero and goes up through 9.

10. What happens when an Exception occurs inside of a try block, and there is

a catch block that handles this sort of exception?

    A> The program terminates(crashes)

    B> An error message is displayed and the program continues.

    C> The program executes the catch block.

Correct answer: C

If an exception happens in a try block the catch block will be executed.

11. Which index item(i.e. array[index item]) do arrays start with?

    A>   0
    B>   1
    C>   double

Correct answer: A

In Java arrays, the starting array index is zero.

12. How do you know when a bubble sort is done?

A>   It is done when you reach the last element of an array

B>   It is done when it finds the first pair of elements that does not need to be swapped.

C>   It is done when it makes it through the array with no swaps.

Correct answer: C

A bubble sort is done when there are no more swaps to be made.

13. What is true of instance variables in properly written Object Oriented Program (OOP) programs?

A>   They should be only accessed through getters/setters

B>   Nothing is wrong with public variables.

C>   Public variables are okay, but you must make them static as well.

Correct answer: A

All class variables should be accessed through getters/setters.

14. What would be the output of the following?

```
String str="Java";
System.out.println( str.charAt(0) );
```

A>   Nothing, it would throw an out of bounds error.

B>   J

C>   a

Correct answer: B

The above code displays the first character of the string, which is "J".

15. How far would the following loop count?

```
for(int i=1;i<10;i++)
```

A>   0 to 10.

B>   From 1 to 9.

C>   From 0 to 9.

Correct answer: B

The above loop will count from 1 to 9.

16. What does the Java import statement do?

A> Displays a line of text.

B> Not a valid Java statement.

C> Allows your program to use other classes.

Correct answer: C

The import statement allows your program to use other classes.

17. Are Java variable names case sensitive?

A> Yes.

B> No.

Correct answer: A

Yes, Java is case sensitive.

18. What is the output of the following?

```
String str = "Java";
System.out.println( str.length() );
```

A> 1

B> 2

C> 3

D> 4

E> Nothing, an exception would be thrown.

Correct answer: D

The string "Java" is 4 characters long.

19. Which of the following makes use of Java's single-line comment?

A>

Comment line 1

#comment line 2

B>

// Comment line 1

// Comment line 2

C>

– Comment line 1

– Comment line 2

D>

/* Comment line 1

Comment line 2 */

Correct answers: B

The single line comment in Java is //, answer D is an example of the multi-line comment.

20. How do you create an array of 10 int's?

A> int x[] = new int[10];

B> int x() = new int(10);

C> int x[10];

Correct answers: A

Answer A has the correct syntax to create an array.

21. Is the following code correct (i.e. will not throw an exception)?

```
int x[];
x = new int[10];
x[10] = 5;
```

A> Yes.

B> No.

Correct answers: B

The code creates a 10 length array. This array ranges from 0 to 9. So accessing element 10 is out of bounds and will throw an exception.

22. What happens when you pass a bad number (i.e. "33jj2") to the Integer. parseInt method?

A>   A NumberFormatException is thrown.

B>   The method would return 0.

C>   The method would return -1.

D>   The method would return null.

Correct answer: A

If Java cannot parse the number, a NumberFormatException will be thrown.

23. If the variable str contains a string and the variable d contains a double, how do you convert str into a double?

A>   d = str;

B>   d = val(str);

C>   d = Double.parseDouble(str);

Correct answer: C

To convert to a double use Double.parseDouble

24. What is the purpose of the substr method of the String class?

A> It subtracts a string.

B> It gets the length of the string.

C> It can be used to break the string into smaller pieces

Correct answer: C

Substring takes substrings of a string, thus breaking it into smaller pieces.

25. How large is the following array? String str[15]

A> Not valid, you don't declare a string in Java with a length.

B> 15

C> 14

Correct answer: A

The proper way to create a string array of size 15 is:

String str[] = new String[15];

APPENDIX C: CHAPTER REVIEW ANSWERS

Answers for Chapter 1

1. What do you call a programming language that will run on many different computer systems, such as Windows, Macintosh and Linux?

Cross Platform.

2. Which company produced Java?

Sun Microsystems.

3. Is Java Object Oriented or Cross platform?

Java is both object oriented and cross platform.

4. What other language does Java's source code resemble?

Java's source code resembles C and C++ source code.

5. What other programming language is often used in place of applets?

Flash is often used in place of applets.

Answers for Chapter 2

1. What is the command to compile the source file "MyProgram. java".

javac MyProgram.java

2. What is contained in a .class file.

Compiled Java code that is ready to be executed.

3. What is the command to compile, and the command to run the Java source file "RunMe.java".

javac RunMe.java
java RunMe

4. What is a program that can be used to edit Java source files?

Notepad, or any text editor can be used to edit Java source files.

5. What must be done to a Java source file before it can be ex-ectued/ran?

Java source files must first be compiled, before they can be ran.

Answers for Chapter 3

1. What is the primary difference between double and long?

A double allows for a floating point, a long does not.

2. What datatype would you use to store the number of students in a class?

A short, int or byte. Because the number of students would not require floating point.

3. What datatype would you use to store someone's hourly wage (i.e. $12.50)?

To store an hourly wage use float or double, because it will need decimal places.

4. **Is String a primitive data type? Why or why not?**

A string is NOT a primitive datatype. It is an object because a string has methods and properties (i.e. str.length()).

5. **What is the purpose of the final keyword?**

Putting the final keyword in front of a variable makes the variable constant.

Answers for Chapter 4

1. **How do you read a number from the user?**

First read a string, then convert the string to a number.

2. **What is the difference between print and println?**

The println method prints a line and carriage return. The print method prints only the line, no carriage return.

3. **What happens if a "bad number" is passed to a method such as Integer.parseInt?**

A bad number will cause the parse function to throw an InvalidNumberException.

4. **How do you handle "bad numbers" properly in a Java program?**

The proper way to handle a "bad number" is to put the parse function inside of a try/catch and catch the NumberFormatException.

5. **What is the purpose of a try/catch block?**

The try/catch block allows you to catch exceptions that would have otherwise crashed your program.

Answers for Chapter 5

1. What are if/else ladders often replaced with?

If/else ladders can often be replaced by switch/case blocks.

2. If no case statement matches what happens?

If there is a default, then that is executed, otherwise execution leaves the switch statement.

3. How do you compare two strings in Java?

To compare strA and strB use strA.equals(strB)

4. Is it possible to make it through an if/else statement and execute neither the if nor else body?

No, that is not possible.

5. How do you use a switch/case with a String?

You can't.

Answers for Chapter 6

1. Is there anything wrong with the following class?

```
public class MyClass
{
  public void test()
  {
    System.out.println("Test");
  }

  public static void main(String args[])
  {
    test();
  }
}
```

Yes, it is trying to call a non-static method (test) from the static method (main). You can't call a non-static method from a static method.

2. What will be the output of this program? Why?

```
public class MyClass
{
  public static void test(int i)
  {
    i = i + 1;
  }

  public static void main(String args[])
  {
    int i = 10;
    test(i);
    System.out.println("i is " + i );
  }
}
```

It will output "i is 10". This is because the method test only modifies the local variable "i" and is not reflected back in main.

3. What is the effect of placing the keyword "static" in front of a local variable?

It will cause the local variable to keep its value, even between function calls.

4. Do the terms class and object mean the same thing? If not, what is the difference.

No a class is a type of something, an object is an instance of a class.

5. Can the main method access instance variables directly?

No, because instance variables are not static.

Answers for Chapter 9

1. What will be the output from the following loop?

```
for( int i = 1; i<10; i++ )
{
  System.out.println( i );
}
```

1
2
3
4
5
6
7
8
9

2. What will be the output from the following loop?

```
int i = 2;
while( i<20 )
{
      System.out.println( i );
      i = i + 5;
}
```

2
7
12
17

3. What will be the output from the following loop?

```
int i = 100;
do
{
  System.out.println( i );
  i = i + 1;
} while( i<10 );
```

It will output 100.

4. Write a loop (for, while or do/while) that will count from 2 to 10 by twos.

for(int i=2;i<=10;i++)
{
 System.out.println(i);
}

5. Rewrite the following for loop as a while loop.

```
for( int i = 1; i<=10; i++ )
{
  System.out.println( i );
}
```

Rewritten as...

```
int i = 1;
while( i<=10 )
{
  System.out.println( i );
  i++;
}
```

Answers for Chapter 10

1. What will be the output from the following code?

```
String str = "Hello World"
System.out.println( str.subString(2,2) );
```

Nothing. This displays everything from 2 up to but not including 2.

2. What will be the output from the following code?

```
String str = "Java";
System.out.println( str.charAt(1) );
```

The letter a.

3. What will be the output from the following code?

```
String str = "Hello World";
System.out.println( str.indexOf(' ') );
```

The number five.

4. What is the difference between a string and a character? What would you store in a string? A character?

A string is a series of characters. A character might store a gender, such as m or f. A string would store someone's name.

5. What is the result of running the following code?

```
String str = "Java";
System.out.println( str.charAt(4) );
```

This would throw an out of bounds error. The valid indexes for the string are 0 to 3.

Answers for Chapter 11

1. What are the three steps necessary to use an array?

Declare, instantiate and initialize.

2. The following code would like to create an array of size 10 and set every array element to 5. Does it accomplish this?

```
public class MyClass
{
  public static void main(String args[])
  {
    int a[] = new int[10];
    for(int i = 0; <10; i++ )
      a[i] = 5;
  }
}
```

Yes, it succeeds.

3. What does the following code try to do? Is it correct?

```
public class MyClass
{
  public static void main(String args[])
  {
    int a[] = new int[10];
    a[10] = 10;
  }
}
```

This code trys to set the last element of an array to 10. This is incorrect, because the array is 10 in length. So valid ranges are from 0 to 9.

4. What must be done to remove one single element of an array?

A loop should be used to copy the element after the one to be deleted. For example, if the array were of length 5, and you wanted to delete element 3, you would first copy element 4 to 3, then copy element 5 to 4. Finally, you would decrease the variable, that holds the size of the array, by one.

5. What index do arrays start at?

zero

Answers for Chapter 12

1. How do you swap the values of two variables?

Copy the first variable to a temp variable. Then copy the second variable to the first. Finally copy the temp variable to the second variable.

2. Describe how the bubble sort works.

The bubble sort examines a list pair-by-pair. If a pair is out of order, its members are swapped. This continues until the bubble sort makes it through with no swaps.

3. Write out the bubble sort stepwise results when sorting the following list of numbers?

4 2 3 5 1

The following steps are necessary.

2 4 3 5 1, end of first round
2 3 4 5 1, end of second round
2 3 4 1 5, end of third round
2 3 1 4 5, end of fourth round
2 1 3 4 5, end of fifth round
1 2 3 4 5, sorted on sixth round

4. **What would the following code display?**

```
String strA = "A";
String strB = "B";

System.out.println( strA.compareTo(strB) );
```

A value less than zero.

5. **What role does the temporary variable play in a bubble sort?**

It holds one value out of the way to avoid copying over it.

Answers for Chapter 13

1. **Write the line of code that will declare an "int", named "i" that has default access.**

int i;

2. **Assume a parent and child class are in the same package. Does the child inherit from the parent, or does the parent inherit from the child?**

The child inherits from the parent.

3. **When inheritance occurs in the same package, which access modifiers will be inherited?**

public, default and protected.

4. Write the getters and setters for the following variable:

```
private int myVariable;
```

public int getMyVariable()
{
 return myVariable;
}

public void setMyVariable(int i)
{
 myVariable = i;
}

5. What is wrong with the following code?

```
interface MyInterface
{
    public int myfunction();
}

public class MyClass implements MyInterface
{
    public int myOtherFunction();
}
```

The MyClass class implements the MyInterface interface, but does not implement the myFunction function.

Answers for Chapter 14

1. Briefly describe what the purpose of the toString function is.

The toString function returns the object formatted as a string. It is often used to display the object.

2. Briefly describe what the purpose of the compareTo function is.

The compareTo method is used to compare two objects and determine their order.

3. What is the connection between the bubble sort and the compareTo function?

The compareTo method lets the bubble sort know what order to place the objects in.

4. Is it REQUIRED that each class that you create contain both a toString and compareTo function?

No. However, if you wish to sort objects of this type you should provide a "compareTo". If you wish to display your object as a String, you should provide a toString. However, neither are required.

5. What is printed out for an object that has no toString function?

A number that corresponds to where the object is stored in memory.

Answers for Chapter 15

1. Describe what a confirm dialog box might be used for.

To ask the user a yes/no type question.

2. Describe what an input dialog box might be used for.

To ask the user to input a string.

3. Describe what a message dialog box might be used for.

To display a message to the user.

4. **Describe what an option dialog box might be used for.**

To present several choices to the user.

5. **What happens if the user clicks cancel for the input dialog?**

A null is returned.

INDEX

Printed in the United Kingdom by
Lightning Source UK Ltd., Milton Keynes
138419UK00001B/30/A